BACK TO

A GUIDE TO SELF-DISCIPLINE
FOR TORY MPs

Mark Leigh and Mike Lepine
on behalf of
The Office of the Chief Whip

HEADLINE

First published in 1994
by HEADLINE BOOK PUBLISHING

10 9 8 7 6 5 4 3 2 1

ISBN 0 7472 4785 4

Designed by Clive Dorman
Typeset from Authors' disks by Clive Dorman & Co.

Printed and bound in Great Britain by
BPC Hazell Books Ltd
A member of
The British Printing Company Ltd

HEADLINE BOOK PUBLISHING
A division of Hodder Headline PLC
338 Euston Road
London NW1 3BH

CONTENTS

FOREWORD

BY JOHN MAJOR, MP

PRIVATE AND CONFIDENTIAL

Dear Fellow Conservative MPs,

You BASTARDS!

There, I've said it and this time I don't care who's
listening.

I don't care if you think this outburst is the natural
gutter language of a common oik who didn't go to public
school. I don't care any more what you think about me. I
know what I think of you.

I am really, really jolly fed up with the lot of you.

There are those among you who thought that my Back to
Basics policy was all about morality. Well, it was...at
first. Well, up to a week after announcing it, anyway. Then
you lot kept getting caught consorting with brazen trollops
and indulging in unmentionable perversions, getting the
good name of the Conservative Party dragged through the
gutter press. Ever since then we've had to patiently
explain that the policy's actually about law and order and
a return to traditional values - that sort of thing.

Well, enough is enough.

Don't think I don't know what's going on in the chambers
and offices of the Palace of Westminster. Just because I
didn't go to a snooty public school like the rest of you,
it doesn't mean I can't comprehend the depths of perversity
some of you are capable of sinking to. I know where the
House of Commons' official hamster mascot went to, believe
me. I can't believe it - but I don't deny the truth of its
horrible fate. Most disagreeable.

However, I do believe that only a minority of the Party
is involved in these despicable antics which are marring my
Back to Basics campaign - and that rumour has exaggerated
the problems we are facing.

I myself am now regularly the target of wild rumour and
speculation.

As leader of the Conservative Party, I am no stranger to being the target of filthy smears and cruel innuendos directed at me on a daily basis from the opposition [By the opposition I mean, of course, Michael Heseltine and Michael Portillo, who I have to fight on an almost daily basis, unlike the Labour Party who can wait until the next general election].

I have also read what certain MPs have been writing about me on the walls of the Palace of Westminster toilet cubicles - and you are getting my dander up. If I ever catch which of you has the yellow crayon in particular, you are in trouble.

Rumours are our greatest enemies - and there is one rumour I feel I must quash immediately.

I am not having a sexual liaison with Bungle the Bear from the children's television programme *Rainbow*.

I don't know where this ridiculous rumour began. I can only surmise that, since my name has been linked with both the words 'bungle' and 'cock-up' quite frequently, the wrong conclusion has been drawn.

Much the same thing happened to start scurrilous and entirely unfounded rumours about myself and my good friend the caterer Ms Claire Latimer. In an interview, I merely said that I had sampled her *veg* on many occasions and found it most agreeable.

Presumably, some inept copy editor did not spot the misprint which subsequently appeared - and a vicious rumour was born. I spent two weeks sleeping in the bath because of that, so believe me when I say I know how it feels to be the victim of false rumours.

Another, particularly distasteful, rumour has linked me with President Clinton's young daughter, Chelsea. As you know, I have Sky Sports in my personal office and, apparently, some of you have been secretly listening in at my door, perhaps hoping to hear me cry in the darkest, loneliest hours of my premiership.

Anyway, some of you have apparently, on occasion heard me shout 'Up Chelsea!' and thought this to reflect some base desire on my part. Worse, I have been heard crying 'Come on Chelsea!' - and the conclusions the more

vulgar of you have drawn from
this particular phrase are
quite despicable.

   Rumour. Our greatest enemy.
I am a keen supporter of
Chelsea FC and it was my
team's progress which I have
been heard to encourage. I
have no sexual feelings
towards Chelsea Clinton
whatsoever. Nothing could be
further from my mind. Nothing.
Well, obviously, congress with
goats. That would be further from my mind. And gymnastic
sex with members of the Ukrainian Parliament in a giant
grain silo inexplicably full of sticky thick Marmite.
That too would be further from my mind.

   Whatever the precise mental topography, I do not wish
to have sex with President Clinton's daughter. Nothing
would be worse for Anglo-American relations than were I
to be caught in flagrante delicto with Chelsea Clinton.

   Rumour has even linked me with Her Majesty the Queen.
Just because I get along with Her Majesty better than
your bloody precious Lady Thatcher ever did, you seem to
think something inappropriate is going on. Let me set the
record straight about the last Christmas party at the
Palace. Yes, there was mistletoe. Yes, Her Majesty did
say, 'pucker up, Prime Minister' and yes, the Whitney
Houston ballad 'I Will Always Love You' WAS playing at
the time. But that is the extent of the truth in the
story. The part about the broom cupboard, the royal
sceptre and the peanut butter spread is totally untrue
and could only be the product of minds twisted by our
public school system. Her Majesty and I enjoyed a full
and frank exchange of views. Not tongues.

   There are other rumours presently in circulation which
must be quashed here and now, lest they escape these
privileged walls and find themselves in the public domain
where they might cause this proud Party untold damage.

   Douglas Hurd did NOT lose a testicle in Korea.

Edwina Currie did NOT use to be Jeremy Thorpe [Apart from the eyebrows, the smouldering dark good looks and certain items in their wardrobes, I really fail to see any resemblance].

These rumours must cease!

Why don't you make up stories about Michael Heseltine for a change? I suppose that's a rhetorical question. I know why. You like him better than me, don't you? Because he went to public school and I didn't. He's 'one of you'.

Now, I have no choice but to put my foot down, as my hero Neville Chamberlain would have done in my place.

I've asked the Office of the Chief Whip to produce this splendid guidebook setting straight, once and for all, what I mean by Back to Basics and how I expect you to conduct your affairs - not that I mean you should have any, of course. I expect you to read it - and take it as the final word on Back to Basics from your leader.

Only by following this sensible advice carefully can the Party hope to escape any future scandals.

Remember, I mean what I say (except when it comes to taxation, benefits, Europe and the NHS) and I will be very cross indeed if you continue to ignore me. Oh yes.

JOHN MAJOR

PS. Whatever you do, don't let this book out of your sight. Not even for a moment. The last thing we want is someone getting hold of it and making a copy. Next thing you know, we'd see it in all the bookshops (probably with a cover taking the mickey out of me, I wouldn't be surprised).

PPS. I hope you like the cartoons I have had especially commissioned to accompany this publication. Since most of you never seem to read anything more demanding than *Viz* or *The Beano*, I thought they would make this document more appealing to you.

INTRODUCTION TO THIS VOLUME

BY THE OFFICE OF THE CHIEF WHIP

The Conservative Party has always stood for traditional family values. However, as is well known within close Party circles, a number of its members consistently indulge in practices, habits and fetishes which are at odds with the values of ordinary, right-thinking people.

The Prime Minister has asked the Office of the Chief Whip to produce an extensive information document explaining to all members of the Parliamentary Conservative Party how his Back to Basics initiative applies to them.

This is having a serious effect on our standing among the voters. The results of this recent, highly confidential, nationwide poll conducted on behalf of the Party shows exactly what the British public currently thinks of us.

What the British public currently thinks of us

Who would make the best job of running this country?

	%
The Labour Party	46.0
The Liberal Democrats	15.0
The Nolan Sisters	14.2
Sooty and Sweep	13.8
A pile of dead voles	8.1
Whoever thought up *Noel's House Party*	1.9
British Rail	0.6
The Conservative Party	0.4

With which of the following do you most associate the Conservative Party?

	%
Strong leadership	0.1
A firm stance on Europe	0.9
Law and order	1.2
Low taxation	0.0
Full employment	0.0
Traditional British values	1.9
Adultery	37.2
Sex with vegetables	19.7
Men dressed as ladies	6.4
Mutual masturbation sessions	2.0
Golden showers	8.0
Bondage	14.8
Hot male-on-male action	4.2
Unthinkable barnyard antics	3.6

How likely are you to vote Conservative in the next general election?

	%
Certain	1.2
Highly likely	3.4
Likely	4.2
Uncertain	6.1
Not likely	14.3
Very unlikely	18.0
Extremely unlikely	25.7
You must be joking!	20.0
I'd rather top myself	3.2
I'd rather top myself, the wife, the kids and the budgie	3.9

With what would you trust a typical Conservative MP?

	No	Yes
Your son	94%	6%
Your daughter	89%	11%
Your wife/husband	99%	1%
Your hamster	72%	28%
Your fruit bowl	62%	38%
Your paypacket	100%	0%

What do you believe the typical Conservative MP is most concerned about?

	%
Education	0.0
Housing	0.0
His constituents	0.0
Shady financial deals	20.6
Marsupials	2.4
Getting his end away	41.7
Advanced auto-erotic techniques	10.3
Being caught at it	25.0

Which of these tactics should the Conservative Party employ to increase its popularity before the next general election?

	%
Resign	85
Die in a fiery maelstrom	94
Bring back Margaret Thatcher	85
Sack John Major	54
Stop bonking assorted tarts and actresses	99
Rig the election	78
Call itself the Labour Party and hope to get voted in by accident	45

Back to Basics sets out the real meaning of John Major's policy and how you can do your part to live up to the high moral values we intend the country to adopt. For simplicity, this document will take the form of a simple question and answer session between a typical Parliamentary backbencher and a senior member of the Office of the Chief Whip – a form of debate familiar to everyone in Parliament. This is an example of how it works:

Hello. I'm a typical Conservative backbench MP. Tell me, what does Back to Basics mean?

It means that we, as MPs, must always adopt the highest moral standards in everything we do. We must set an example and appear as paragons of virtue to the public.

Piss off!

No. Really.

I thought we'd fobbed off the plebs by saying that Back to Basics applied to something boring and dull and oiky, like transport or education or Sunday trading or something.

Sorry. It didn't work. They still believe it refers to MPs' personal behaviour...

It's all the fault of that jumped-up grammar school boy, Major! It's time we had a leadership struggle.

At present, John Major is our leader and forms our policies. Back to Basics is at the heart of our policies.

Why? Why pick morality as a key issue when he knows we're all at it with anything – animal, vegetable or mineral?

John Major is a shrewd politician. He has realised that the Conservative Party must champion a popular cause if we are to win the next election – and since our policies for education, foreign affairs, finance, healthcare and law and order were all so inept, there wasn't much left to us that we could claim to champion over the other parties.

This would never have happened if we were still the Party who wanted to keep all the nuclear missiles. We had defence to make us popular back then.

That was before the fall of the Soviet Empire...

Put back the Berlin Wall, that's what I say. Bring back the Cold War. The Red Threat! They were great days. The public were terrified, and there was a swarthy, sexy KGB agent on every block offering us cash and all the boy scouts we could eat in exchange for a few policy documents...

The PM will brook no further arguments. The rules set out in this Back to Basics policy document apply to everyone, from the PM and the Cabinet down to the lowest and most humble of backbenchers, like yourself!

Lowest? How dare you! My daddy owns Rio Tinto Banana.

Pardon?

Zinc. Rio Tinto Zinc. Not banana. Not at all. No fruit in my underwear. Or anywhere else. Never even saw a banana until I was thirty-five.

Do you understand the issues? And the stakes?

Of course.

Good.

Fancy a threesome?

TEMPTATION

SKELETONS IN THE CLOSET

With one or two very notable exceptions, members of the Tory Party have enjoyed the benefits of a public school education.

While the educational and societal benefits of such an education are not in dispute, Mr Major has expressed extreme disquiet in private about the high incidence of sexual perversion at boys' boarding schools, disguised as initiation ceremonies, pranks, japes, high-jinks, traditions and sports days.

Forewarned is forearmed, so Mr Major wants to know, from each of you, if you participated in any such activities during your public school days which might give rise to scandal in the future.

What sort of activities, precisely, are you referring to?
Games played after 'lights out' of an...experimental nature... which helped to determine the course of your later sexual development. Like *Breakfast at Tiffany's.*
Breakfast at Tiffany's? *I don't remember that one. How's that played?*
Well, you know what a *Pearl Necklace* is...
Oh! We called that Supper at Aspreys.
Whatever you called it at your school, those are the types of 'games' I am referring to.
You mean like the infamous Eton Round the Horn Race...
No. What's that? I went to Charterhouse.
Then you must know the equally infamous Charterhouse Brylcream Trampoline Game...
We didn't play that when I was there. We all played... Monopoly.
Really? Weren't you there at the same time as 'Sperm Bank' Matthews?
No.
What about Gordon 'Hamster' Montgomery? 'Corky' Maximillian? Dickie 'Dickie' Roberts? Roger 'Roger' Llewellyn-Llewellyn? He has his own Harley Street practice now, y'know, darn fine proctologist. Start young, that's what I say...don't be frightened of rolling up your sleeves and getting your hands a bit dirty...
Er...yes. Perhaps we could return to the subject.
Thank you. I almost let the cat out of the bag there. Got a bit carried away. Public school sex games, such as the *Harrow Hide the Tonka Toy Annual Weekend...*
How do you play that?

It's similar to the *Eton Disappearing School Mascot Game*. Why?
No reason. No reason.

...such as the *Harrow Hide the Tonka Toy Annual Weekend* and the *Rugby Pubic Topiary Initiation Ceremony* can be damaging to the developing psyche and lead to the onset of sometimes severe sexual deviation affecting your later professional life, as of course could that most infamous of all public school games, *Jack the Biscuit*...

> **John Major says...**
>
> Er...I'm sorry to interrupt, but I heard someone mention biscuits. Naturally my curiosity was piqued. Piqued-Freened, you could say, if you might excuse the pun...

We were just discussing the notorious public school game called *Jack the Biscuit*, in which young male participants from excellent stock and good families crouch around a biscuit and proceed to...sexually gratify themselves...over it. The last schoolboy to...er...complete the function then pays the forfeit of having to *eat* said biscuit.

> **John Major says...**
>
> Oh. Oh. Oh. How - oh. Speaking as someone renowned for his interest in biscuitry and related delectations, I must express my natural horror and indeed my revulsion, at such a practice.
>
> MPs will know that, when they come to visit me in my office, I always make freely available to them a delicious assortment of biscuits in a charming turquoise biscuit barrel that used to belong to an aunt of mine. MPs are trusted absolutely with the biscuits during the course of the meeting and I have, until now, let the barrel out of my sight during these meetings, supposing my biscuits to be safe from abuses of this nature.
>
> Now I am aware of this practice, things can never be the same. All trust is gone. I might turn

> away to take a telephone call and come back to find
> my Garibaldis violated. Now I come to think of it,
> some of my Huntley and Palmer's pink wafers were a
> bit soggy the last time I sampled them, but I put
> this down to their age. Certainly, I could never
> look upon a Vanilla Cream in the same light
> again...

Don't worry, Prime Minister. This game is only ever played with biscuits from Harrods, not the common or garden varieties you delight in purchasing with your petty cash.

Blast! He found out about the biscuit barrel!

Here are some other popular public school games which you should inform the Prime Minister if you participated in:

* Truth or Consequences
* Kiss Chase [single sex schools only]
* Postman's Knock [ditto]
* Up Periscope!
* First Year Compulsory Penile Teeth Cleaning Ceremonies
* Pass the Wad
* Naked Twister [with or without the cooking oil]
* Identify the Taste
* 3-2-1
* Find the Ferret
* Upstairs, Downstairs
* Squeaky, Piggy, Squeak
* The Glorious Twelfth Beaters Game
* Packing the Brown Valise...
* Whist

Whist? There's nothing wrong with whist!

There is if you play it in just your underpants, sitting astride a First Year's face.

True. True.

So...

They play different games now to the ones we used to play, you know.

Really?

Yes. I went on a special high-level Government fact-finding mission to my old dorm after lights out...

Was that wise?

No. But strangely refreshing.

This is precisely the sort of behaviour that Back to Basics is there to stop.

I'm in love you know. With a little Arabic angel. A cheeky, cherry-cheeked cherub with legs that...

Please. No more!

Why?

It's making me uncomfortable.

He's called Abdhul.

Shut up!

Abdhul Ben Bigboy.

You're making it up!

They call him 'Stretchy' Abdhul...

I don't believe you!

Please yourself.

I might have to. Very soon now. Excuse me...

Would you like a hand?

Whist is an acceptable game – unless
you play it astride a First Year's face

RESEARCHERS AND SECRETARIES

Usually beautiful young girls from good families with brains to match their striking goood looks, Parliamentary researchers and secretaries probably present the single greatest temptation for MPs to stray from the straight and narrow in the course of their political careers.

If you're the sort of sad, little, sexually frustrated man who usually wouldn't even stand a chance with a chloroformed sheep, you are a sitting duck for any ambitious little schemer who thinks she can sleep her way to the top in party politics.

Prior to an interview, there can be early warning signs of trouble ahead – in the form of a sexually alluring CV:

Other Qualifications

Driver's licence, long blonde hair, being double jointed, extensive wardrobe (and props), a figure that would make the Pope sweat buckets.

Hobbies / Interests

Older men (and no complications), weekends by the sea in discreet hotels, collecting thigh length leather boots, exercising my taut, firm, bronzed, well toned body, reading, music.

Previous experience

VERY extensive.

References from previous employers

Mr J K Jones
c/o The Home for the Prematurely Aged
Bournemouth
Dorset

Mr L V Francis
c/o Bluebird Convalescent Home
Rickmansworth
Herts

Mr T Jackson
c/o The Home For The Terminally Shagged
Cromer
Norfolk

Mr R Norman
c/o Intensive Care Ward 7
Cloverdale Hospital
Basingstoke

When you interview an applicant for a job, look out for deliberately provocative answers – like so:

Why did you leave your last job?
My previous employer suffered a fatal heart attack, but I already felt I needed to leave and try out a new position.

Why do you want this job?
My...it's hot in here. Do you mind if I unbutton my blouse...to the waist?

Do you think you could cope with our word processor?
Yes. By the way, aren't the leather chairs in this office sexy? I find leather so...irresistible. They charge the whole of your office with this kind of intense kinetic sexual magnetism that could quite turn a girl's head and make her prey to even the most clumsy of advances from the most physically loathsome of men.

How do you feel about working in a predominantly male environment?
Ever since I left secretarial college I've been under lots of men – so that shouldn't be a problem.

Are there any questions that you'd like to ask about the Conservative Party?
Do you have a stationery cupboard that's soundproof, big enough to wriggle around in a bit and lockable from the inside?

How do you see your career progressing within the Party?
I'm a very ambitious woman and I'd like to think that you'd give me every opportunity to go all the way. Would you like me to perform oral sex on you?

Why can't I have a little naughty fun with a Party employee if I like? We're both consenting adults.
But have you considered why this beautiful young girl is consenting to have sex with you?
Women find power irresistible. I am a powerful politician, with the raw animal smell of 'Leader of the Pack' about me...
...and a paunch and a hairline that's receded so far it's on the back of your neck and teeth that are more disjointed and crooked than Italian politics? Stop living in dreamland. This woman wants you for one purpose only – to advance her career. You will be sucked into her seductive spell.
Sounds great!
You will be under her power completely, at the whim of her mercy. You will find yourself neglecting your Party and constituency duties, composing tender little love letters to her, like the genuine, sordid example reproduced opposite above...

When she's got you into a compromising position, she'll turn the tables on you, like so...
  After a few 'late sessions' and one or two 'working weekends', an industrious girl should be well on her way to compiling her very own 'little brown envelopes' and you will receive a note something like this:

Mistress Jane,

It has been only three days since our exquisite weekend of unending pain in Brighton but I am already longing for the feel of your cruel lash on my defenceless buttocks, and your brutal, brutal tongue telling me I'm unfit even to be an Ulster unionist. And then the feel of cold electrical cable wound tightly round my wrists as I am forced to eat Coco Pops from a dog's bowl while you look on, laughing at my degradation.

How are you fixed for the weekend of the 20th?

Your obedient slave,

Sir ~~████████~~ . p

Dear Sir ████,

I think it's about time we stopped talking about your sad and pathetic desires, and started talking about my promotion — don't you?

Have you heard of 'Candid Camera'? Well a friend of mine took lots of snaps of us, that night you pretended to be Cleopatra — and I pretended to be Judith Chalmers — Remember?

And I have the negatives.

Love

Jane Smith (MS)

P.S. I also kept all the receipts — here's a photocopy if you don't believe me.

Wellingtons Greengrocers & High Class Fruiterers
16-18 Denton Road, Brighton, Sussex BN3 8SC

3 doz. Courgettes   £17.64
1 marrow (large)   £0.85

FUN TIME Party Outfitters
84, Harrovia Mews, Brighton

Hire of schoolgirl outfit,
mortar board, gown & cane   £35.00

The Doverton Hotel

263, St Augustine Road, Brighton, Sussex BG14 8DZ

1 double room with bath and shower, 2 nights....£160.00
14 bottles of Moet & Chandon NV.................£415.00
Oysters for two.................................£ 17.50
Bouquet of flowers..............................£ 25.00
Rare jungle orchids (1 doz).....................£270.00
Replacement leg for bed.........................£ 32.20
Total...£919.70
All figures are inclusive of V

Harrisons Electrical Discount Store
25-29 Haydings Road, Brighton, Sussex BG15 4DS

20 FEET OF 13 AMP
MAINS CABLE   £11-20

Cavalier Sex Shop
48 The Felchings, Brighton, Sussex

2 pkts of Ejaculex 2000 pills
1 jar of XXX Hot Rod cream   £ 9.00
Giant size pkt of Dr. Casanova's   £ 7.50
Keep-It-Up Super Secret Lotion
Book: 'How To Please A Woman In Bed'   £14.99
Naughty Boy red leather stippled   £ 9.99
posing pouch (small)

TOTAL: £19.95

                                            £61.63

- 22 -

You would be stunned by how many MPs in our Party are presently the subject of blackmail demands from researchers and secretaries threatening to spill the beans.

Here is just a sample of the mail we received at Central Office last week.

Attention: CENTRAL OFFICE
  Please promote Jane Smith. She can have my job as MP for Wendover Central if you like, I don't mind. I'd be quite happy to go back to being a mere party worker and sharing an office with thirty other people again and take a £7000 pay cut and lose my Ford Sierra and key to the Commons washroom. Who needs it? I want to be one of the boys again and not some over-paid, over-privileged backbencher who does no work all day.
  Look, I'll pay for the sign to be changed on the office door, and retype the telephone extension list myself, so it won't be any sort of bother for the party and I'm sure Jane Smith will adjust to my position within 25 seconds, so you'll never notice the difference.

MP, ▓▓▓▓▓▓▓

Attention: CENTRAL OFFICE
  Please, please, please promote Jane Smith. I've got five children and I love my wife, really I do, even after twenty five years of marriage.

MP, ▓▓▓▓▓▓▓

Attention: CENTRAL OFFICE
  Please promote Jane Smith. She deserves it out of sheer merit, and not because I'm having it away with her like the rumours say. They're liars, all of them, especially that little tramp Trisha in the typing pool, besmirching the spotless reputation of this innocent, angelic, industrious cherub of a girl who likes nothing better than to work hard and get on, and who certainly doesn't like staying behind after hours to play sexy love games in the stationery cupboard.
  I don't find her attractive anyway: I prefer ugly girls, really, really dead ugly ones with bloated bodies and sickly complexions and legs like concrete traffic bollards, so you see that Jane Smith obviously isn't my type. In fact, I'm gay, and I don't mind admitting it, so anything between Jane Smith and me is completely out of the question.
  In fact, we've never even spoken, let alone spent a weekend of illicit passion in a Brighton Hotel that almost killed me, and all I know about her is how wonderful a worker she is, and how much she deserves promotion.

John C▓▓▓

MP, Smethwick Grange

If we are to take on board Back to Basics, the whole question of secretaries and researchers must be urgently reviewed.

There is a simple way out of this.

There is?

Yes. We could stop employing women as researchers and secretaries altogether.

That's good thinking.

Instead we could hire men to do their jobs. Of course, some of them would have to wear women's clothing – just so no one would spot the fact that we weren't employing women and complain of sexual discrimination.

Perhaps not...

*Temptation could be avoided by hiring only
male research assistants*

Of course, these chaps who we got to dress up as women would have to be quite svelte and slender and feminine to start with and look good in fishnets and stilettos.

I don't think...

And we'd have to call them by girls' names, like Katy and Delores – and we'd have to be prepared to give them a kiss under the mistletoe at Christmas, just to keep up appearances.

Perhaps the present system, with all its pitfalls, is preferable.

I always think that Scandinavian men make the best female impersonators – which is a shame, because darker, more Latino men can look darn good in a tight leather mini-skirt and knitted leg-warmers.

Look, I'll suggest it to the Prime Minister...

Will you? They could wear sarongs...

We'll see. There are, of course, perfectly innocent researchers, assistants and secretaries – and making unwelcomed sexual advances towards them can be just as problematic under Back to Basics as predatory females...

Sexual harassment is just good fun!

No it's not. The last thing any responsible female employee wants to hear from you is something like 'Gillian, come in here please. There's something you really must take down for me'.

Other unacceptable acts of harassment include:

* Putting up a Page 3 calendar. Taking pictures of some of the women in the Party and sticking their faces on to it.

* Writing on the Parliamentary year planner all the dirty weekends you intend having with the girls.

* Asking one of the secretaries for an elastic band. When she asks 'why?', winking and telling her that you've heard it can make you 'last longer'.

* Leaving suggestive telephone messages on girls' desks just like these...

Telephone Message

TO: **STACEY**

While you were out: I HAD A FANTASY ABOUT YOU, ME, THE SECRETARY IN THE NEXT OFFICE, STRAWBERRY BLANCMANGE, 18 OVER-RIPE BANANAS AND FREEFALL PARACHUTING. CAN YOU GUESS WHAT HAPPENED?

From Rt. Hon Member

Telephone Message

TO: Sandra

While you were out: I sniffed your chair and it gave me the horn.

Rt. Hon Member Wood-on-wye

Telephone Message

TO: Helen

While you were out: I dangled it in your Garfield coffee mug!

Rt Hon member South Eddington. X

Telephone Message

TO: Tina

While you were out: Me and the other MPs on the transport policy committee talked about your bosoms.

Rt Hon Member west Landsam.

Telephone Message

TO: JANE

While you were out: I SNEAKED INTO PERSONNEL, TOOK YOUR PHOTO OUT OF THE FILES AND SHOVED IT DOWN THE FRONT OF MY BOXER SHORTS AND SORT OF RUBBED IT ABOUT.

Rt Hon. Member for Richley X

Ah! Now I remember why I became an MP in the first place!

FACT-FINDING MISSIONS

Has the situation changed regarding fact-finding missions?
No. These visits are permitted providing they are relevant to work you are carrying out either for the Party or your constituents.

Will Central Office still fund these trips?
Yes, but with the proviso again that they are legitimate trips for Parliamentary purposes.

Such as?
Oh, the usual business, like visiting some dodgy overseas nuclear waste processing plant to see if it's suitable for use over here. Greasing the palms of oily foreign businessmen to get them to relocate a factory in some godforsaken part of Northern England – you know the sort of thing. Why? Are you thinking of going on one?

Possibly. What about a trip to Amsterdam?
Well, it depends...

Fact-finding missions must be legitimate trips
for Parliamentary purposes

Or Hamburg?

Possibly – but why do you want to go there?

You know, to check on um... er... European farm subsidies. Yes, that's it. To check on the relative subsidy levels and how this affects the overall trade balance of the European Community.

But this information would be readily available just down the corridor in the Commons library...

Is it? Well, the information might be out of date and you can't beat going somewhere in person to check your facts and figures.

Really?

Yes.

Well, how long would this fact-finding mission to, say, Amsterdam, last?

Oh, about five nights. I mean five days. Days and nights, actually.

I see. But there's no EC Department of Agriculture based in Amsterdam – or Hamburg.

There could be. There could very well be a Department of Agriculture in both those cities but you don't know about it.

Are you wasting my time?

No... well what about Bangkok? Yes, that's it. A week in Bangkok.

But Thailand isn't even in Europe, let alone the EC!

The Philippines. That's it. Manilla's where I want to go.

Listen, are you by any chance wanting to go round some of the world's most famous red light areas in order to evaluate whether there's a need to legalise prostitution in this country?

Why do you ask?

Well, we received a similar application last month and John Major turned it down flat.

I suppose that means a visit to an isolated farmyard in the Turkish mountains is also out of the question?

Yes. The Rt Honourable Members for Higley Park and Cartlesham West are already on a fact-finding mission there – and they were due back six weeks ago.

Jammy sods!

APPLICATION FOR FUNDING FOR A FACT-FINDING MISSION

REJECTED

NAME: Sir Iain Carstairs-Tupp
POSITION: Rt Hon Member for Eastleigh Green
PLANNED DESTINATION: All the red light districts in the world
DURATION OF VISIT: Open ended (similar to how I'll end up)
OBJECTIVE: The oldest profession in Britain has had no central government control in its entire history. My research is intended to pave the way for the standardisation of charges and services and to protect consumers who currently have no recourse to law in cases of dissatisfaction. Or crabs.

I have already outlined possible ways to regulate this industry; this fact-finding mission is required to ratify these proposals.

PLEASE STATE BELOW THE SUBJECTS YOU WILL BE INVESTIGATING:

1. The rationalisation of services and charges
There is currently no BS 5750 standard for sexual favours offered. For example, a 'Quick One' in Manchester is appreciably longer than a 'Quick One' in Bradford. Similarly, on the subject of 'Manual Relief', in Hull, a 'Hand Shandy' uses all fingers and includes unlimited free Kleenex, while only the thumb and forefinger are employed in Bournemouth and many other South Coast towns. Apparently.

2. Maintaining standards of service
To ensure that brothels offer the required level of service, yearly written and oral examinations will be mandatory.

3. Licensing of brothels
To designate a licensed brothel a government approved red light must be displayed during opening hours. (Until now some lights have been orange, some a deep purple while others were just white bulbs covered with red Quality Street wrappers - none of which seem to be commensurate with the new image we are discussing for this industry).

4. Union Activity
Prostitutes have already discussed forming a 'Union Of Prostitutes, Whores, Saucy Women and Fellatrixes' and it is expected that my rationalisation plan will expedite this move.
It is anticipated that this union will be affiliated to the current 'Association Of Manual Workers'.

5. Creation of a Cabinet post responsible for prostitution
The best way to regulate this industry would be to appoint a 'Minister for Prostitution' (the best candidate for this post is likely to be the MP who instigated this fact finding mission in the first place).

6. Excise Duty
VAT will be payable only on sexual acts involving actual sexual penetration. ('Hand Relief', going 'All Round The World', 'Felching', enemas, 'Golden Showers', 'Gilding the Ferret', 'Launching The Lifeboat', 'Smudging', 'Knitting' and 'Shampooing the Carpet' would all be zero-rated - as would 'Doing a Prince Andrew').

ENTERTAINMENT AND SOCIALISING

MPs enjoy a hectic whirl of social events – parties, balls, official functions.

Beware! This is where temptation lurks, where, far away from the rigid strictures of our day to day duties in Parliament, the temptation is to unwind, let your guard down, relax...

...Get pissed and shag some model.

Exactly. You see the danger. In future, John Major expects you all to be more careful about the type of social function you choose to attend. Prevention is better than cure.

Safe events to accept invitations to would include:

* Dinner with your parents
* The Ceylon Tea Blenders Guild
* Your local WRVS coffee morning
* A recital of Bach's Organ music
* A tour around Mr Kipling's automated cake manufacturing plant
* The dedication of a new locomotive

Dangerous events to accept invitations to would include:

* Page 3 Girl of the Year contest
* Page 7 Fella of the Year contest
* The opening of a new rectal thermometer factory
* Any gathering advertising for 'broad-minded AC/DC couples'
* Any cattle auction
* Any other event involving the parading of livestock
* The Turkish Trade Delegation's 'Getting To Know You' jacuzzi fancy dress party
* The Syrian Ambassador's son's fifth birthday party
* Any other event that involves young Middle Eastern boys and a bouncy castle
* The 'judge the marrow' contest at a local fete

I've got an invitation here to the world's largest boy scout jamboree. Can I go to that?

No.

Please...

I'm sorry, but the temptation would be just too great. Stick to more orthodox functions as part of your commitment to Back to Basics. And, while you're at even the 'safest' of functions, do try to behave by observing the following simple guidelines.

Things to do:

* Make polite conversation
* Promote Conservatism
* Impress people with your breadth of political acumen
* Support the present leadership
* Stay sober

Things not to do:

* Spew up down another guest's dinner suit
* Spew up in a flower pot
* Spew up on the stairs in a desperate race for the toilet
* Have sex in the bedroom on top of the coats [which, in all probability, someone's already spewed up on anyway]
* A slow striptease to a string quartet
* Challenge a certain European VIP to a 'light your own fart' contest [You know who you are...]

Polite conversation at official functions makes a positive impression. Rude, obnoxious and boorish behaviour tarnishes the Party image. Stuck for words?

Here are some perfectly acceptable phrases:

* I thought the after dinner speaker made some excellent points about Croatia
* Proportional representation, by its very nature, can only lead to the politics of compromise
* Tactical voting pleases no one; it's the politics of protest
* John Major is the man to lead us into the next general election

On the other hand, here are some recently overheard phrases which the Prime Minister tells me he does not want to hear his MPs uttering again.

* I'm an MP. How about it?
* Hey, wow, I can see your nips!
* Fancy playing 'Poll the electorate'?
* Who's this? 'Hello, I'm really, really boring...'
* Well, that's that ruddy function out of the way; let's mingle our love essences.
* Off! Off! Off! Off!
* Look, right, I'm telling you, it's so big it could be a bloody constituency all on its own. In fact, I'm its MP. I represent the constituency of Penis Central. It's got a huuuuuge...enormous...huuuuge working majority. Oh dear, I'm going to be sick...

I remember saying that. Stupid cow. Went off with the Right Honourable Member for Bournemouth Central in the end.

There are times when you will want to entertain your own guests, and throw your own official functions; once again, discretion should be used at every stage.

It is a good idea to invite guests because they have:

* Influence
* Connections with industry and commerce in your constituency
* Worked hard for charitable causes

* Important things to say
* Large donations they want to make to the Party

It is not a good idea to invite guests because they have:

* A 44DD chest
* A reputation as a 'goer'
* A really funny speech impediment you can mimic
* A leather catsuit and a great collection of ropes
* A gorgeous wife you can try and get off with during the course of the evening

If you are thinking of hosting your own official function, our leader can offer you a host of helpful hints and tips.

John Major says...

Both Norma and I pride ourselves on our social skills.

When entertaining guests, we always find it a good idea to have plenty of biscuits available in case they are peckish. When entertaining someone you do not know well – or a large gathering – a Crawfords selection box may please even the most discerning of palates. I remember once the Emir of Dubai being quite pleasantly surprised by one of those ones with jam in the middle.

As for music, well it largely depends upon your visitors. We find *James Last Plays Great TV Theme Tunes* is well received by foreign royalty, while ambassadors and other overseas diplomats seem perfectly content to listen over and over again to our cherished Tony Monopoly album.

Party games are always a good way of breaking the ice at such functions, especially if they are with representatives of a hostile foreign power. While I confess that when I suggested I Spy to a visiting Russian trade delegation, they all made their excuses and disappeared with a strange rapidity, most of Norma and my games go down exceedingly well. Different peoples excel at different games, you will find.

Nigerian visitors, for example, enjoy all the fun and excitement of Musical Chairs, while representatives from more southern African states prefer Simon Says and – should you have boxed games under your coffee table as we do – a few quick, nerve-racking rounds of Ker-plunk! are looked upon with great favour by the Central American republics. Buckeroo! is popular with most Scandinavians and anyone from The Gabon cannot fail to be impressed by the wisdom and wonder of The Magic Robot.

Other devices I find useful for breaking the ice at our social gatherings include handing out comedy hats and all sitting around in a circle repeating our names to get to know one another.

Try these useful tips to help your next official engagement go with a swing!

This is no fun. If I can't enjoy myself as an MP, I'm going to resign my seat.

You can't.

Why not?

You're in a marginal constituency.

So, I can go to that boy scout jamboree after all?

If you promise to be good.

Good? I'll be bloody outstanding!

MI5 AND THE SECURITY SERVICES

What's wrong with our security services? They're meant to be on our side, aren't they?

Sadly this is no longer true. In years gone by, they would use their dirty tricks only on enemies of the state – like the Labour Party.

Now they consider anyone fair game. If they can nobble Charles and Di, they can get you too.

Why?

Different factions within the security services appear to have different agendas. One group within MI5 who were at Cambridge studying the arts together seem to be involved in a large 'outing' exercise. Others are determined to destabilise our present Government because it is not sufficiently right wing for their tastes at present. Revealing us as hypocrites during our Back to Basics campaign could conceivably bring the Government down.

Things were much better in years gone by, when only Labour were targeted. Everyone remembers how MI5 tried to bring about the downfall of the Wilson Government, by faking evidence to show that Harold Wilson, far

from being a mild-mannered, family man, was, in fact, a blood-crazed werewolf who wrote 'STOP ME BEFORE I KILL AGAIN' in sheep's blood in his office. Denis Healey's career was almost brought to an abrupt end when he was framed for being one of the living dead. [It was this same tactic that eventually disposed of Michael Foot]

Good God! What sort of tactics are these bounders employing in their nefarious schemes against Tories nowadays?

MI5 'dirty tricks' range from the quite minor – ringing your doorbell and running away – to fully fledged surveillance operations and entrapments.

One of MI5's favourite techniques is to break into MPs' London flats and search for evidence that you are involved in activities which might pose a threat to national security.

Remember, with MI5 you are dealing with largely public school types like yourselves, so their behaviour will be instantly recognisable.

Here are some tell-tale signs that MI5 has burgled your flat:

* Your ornaments have been tastefully rearranged to improve the aesthetic ambience of the room.
* Your washing up has been done and neatly racked.
* Your underwear drawer has been extensively rifled. At least one pair shows evidence of being worn and another of being placed over the head and vigorously rubbed about.
* All tubes of lubricating creams and gels are missing.
* There are stiletto marks back and forth across your shagpile.
* Your poster of Keanu Reeves is missing.

What else do they do?

Phone tapping is another favourite technique, collecting evidence against you from incriminating phone calls.

Some sure signs that your phone is being bugged:

* A 'BT telephone engineer' has recently visited you to inspect your phone [when did you ever see a real BT engineer?].
* Strange 'clicking' and 'tapping' noises on the line.
* Muffled sniggering on what sounds like a crossed line.
* Echoed heavy breathing on the line when you dial 'Spank my Panties' or any other 0898 number...

If you have reason to suspect that your telephone is being tapped, do not use
it for private calls.

What should I do?

Use a public call box instead.

*What? How can I dial up 'Spank my Panties' from a public phonebooth? I
won't be able to...you know...with the rolled up newspaper and the bar of
moistened soap. And right in the middle of the call some oik will want to use
the box and I'll be frustrated and grumpy and probably rebel against the
Government the next day.*

By far the most dangerous tactic they use is to deliberately get you to
incriminate yourself. MI5 presently runs a number of covert operations,
designed to trap the unwary MP. The ones we know of at Central Office
include:

* The Parliamentarian Massage Parlour
* The Chihuahua of the Month Club
* Boyz-R-Us
* XXXX Escorts [Oriental girls a speciality]
* The Official Hitler's Bunker Re-enactment Society and Jacuzzi
* The Alternative London Dungeon experience
* The Hampstead & Belsize Park Fruit Delivery Service

So none of them is genuine?

No.

I suppose I'll have to send the chihuahua back then.

With all the speed you can muster – but it may already be too late!

I tell you – right now, I'm feeling a prize prick.

Good. I'm pleased you're starting to see the error of your ways.

No that wasn't an observation. It was actually a statement of fact.

Oh. Stop it and pay attention!

If you do not fall for any of these tricks, they may send an operative over
to seduce you.

A typical MI5 set-up is easy to spot, if you remember the following:

* Boy scouts no longer go from door to door offering 'Bob a Job' –
especially not with a knowing wink accompanied by pelvic gyrations.
Modern day boy scouts do NOT wear short trousers and – as far as we are
aware – no scout has ever worn a waspie as part of their official uniform.

I did.
I said 'official uniform'.

* Stray dogs clad in leather studded 'doggy coats' do not ring door bells.
Someone has to do it for them...
* Drop-dead-beautiful 18-year-old girls do not normally find 50-year-old,
four-eyed, fat and flabby, balding sweaty types a turn-on or suggest going
to bed as soon as they sit down next to you.
* The Chippendales do not need to practise in your flat. These men are
frauds!
* A horse that comes to your door and suggests vigorous sex is most likely
to be two MI5 agents in a pantomime horse costume, one of whom is willing
to make the ultimate sacrifice for national security.

But beware! Sometimes those who are out to trap you may not be MI5 agents – but their KGB rivals. They use many similar tactics in their attempts to subvert MPs – but it is now very simple to tell if an MP is in the pay of the Russians:

* He's always desperately short of cash...
* ...But not of turnips.
* He is often the proud owner of a new [or newish] Lada Riva.
* Instead of stealing defence documents, he carefully puts a few jam tarts in a tissue in the Commons canteen for his Russian controllers to sell back in Moscow.
* The girl he has been seduced by looks uncannily like Arnold Schwarzenegger – only taller.
* If you go through his wallet, it's full of IOUs written in Cyrillic.
* He's always sticking things into holes in trees.

The Right Honourable Member for Harrow North does that. Is he a KGB double agent?

No. He's a pervert.

You know, it's jolly brave of you...

What is...

Saying all these terrible things about MI5. They're bound to come after you now, you know.

Oh. Er...I just forgot this vital piece of information which I should have included earlier on...

Why we should be jolly proud of our secret service:

* They're an equal opportunities employer, employing more gay people than any other branch of government or industry.
* They manage to keep their exploits so secret that most of us believe they're actually doing nothing at all.
* They certainly nobbled Charles and Di.
* Thank God they're there, just in case it looks like Labour might win a General Election.

* Contrary to popular belief, their agents do not have a licence to kill – but they are permitted to give any spies they uncover a jolly stiff telling off.
* They always used to beat the KGB, Mossad and the CIA at cricket in the one-day Secret Service Test Series.
* They keep excellent tabs on dangerous radicals like vegetarians and animal rights campaigners, who are a much bigger threat to the status quo than the forces of Bolshevism.
* They're such good losers; how British...

THE POWER OF THE PRESS

You may be the most upright and moral MP in Parliament, but could you stand up to real temptation?

Try me.

Don't test your resolve. It's nearly always a mistake.

No, I meant try me. You Chief Whip's Office johnnies really turn me on. It's the authority thing...

Sorry, under Back to Basics I cannot enter into anything with you.

Not even this?

No. Not even that. Now pull your pants back up and let us progress onto the topic of the press...

The press say that they are the guardians of the public interest. What they really mean is that sex and hypocrisy sells newspapers. Back to Basics has made us sitting ducks for the press. They smell blood and they're moving in for the kill by trying to tempt MPs into compromising situations.

Beware of national newspapers attempting to set you up...

How can you tell when a newspaper is trying to set you up?

Unlike members of MI5, most journalists haven't had the benefit of an Oxbridge education and so are far more likely to entice you with women, instead of hunky black men or bags of fruit.

Where do these shameless hussies that they use come from?

They are usually aspiring actresses or models, trying to make a name for themselves.

No, I mean, what are their actual addresses and telephone numbers?

You'll be forced to go...

But what a way to go! As duly erected MP for Minge Central!

If you meet a strange woman who invites you back to her place, decline.

No.

You really should.

Not on your life!

Well, in that case, be very alert for anything strange which may start to occur.

Beware of it? I'm looking forward to it!

You really don't appreciate the possible gravity of the situation, do you? Before a newspaper will dare to print a story, it must get incontrovertible proof – like videotape or audio tape records of what went on between you and the woman.

Here is a typical account of a sexual encounter as engineered by a national newspaper, taken from several real-life case studies. See if you can spot the warning signs:

MP: Nice bedroom you have here...

WOMAN: Let's do it right here and now...like rutting animals!

MP: Yeah. All right then. Just let me phone my wife and tell her that Parliament's sitting late tonight...

WOMAN: Forget her! She could never do for you what I'm going to do for you...unless she's double jointed.

MP: All right.

WOMAN: You know what would really turn me on? If you were to wear women's clothing and then I'll put on a Long John Silver costume and a John Smith Face Mask – and then we'll do it six times a night, employing the liberal use of a banana.

MP: Phew!

WOMAN: No – don't turn the lights out! It's better when they're on. Oh, that matching bra and garter set looks so good on you. It goes so well with my Chelsea football supporters' cap.

MP: This is fabulous!

WOMAN: You know what would really turn me on now? If you were to face that wardrobe over there and keep perfectly still for a few moments...

MP: Certainly. Why, my dear?

WOMAN: It turns me on like you wouldn't believe!

MP: What, me staring directly at the wardrobe?

WOMAN: Yes!!! Oh God, Yessss!

MP: All right then...

WOMAN: Oh God, that's just so good! You looking straight at the wardrobe. I'm ready for it now, lover boy!

MP: Er...are there any other items of furniture you'd like me to look directly at...you know...to get you going. That dressing table over there for example. I could look at that for a while...

WOMAN: Forget the furniture! I'm aching for you! Tell me all your state secrets! Whisper hot defence plans in my ears. Make pillow talk of immense strategic importance!

MP: What? Why?

WOMAN: You haven't slept with many women, have you? Don't you realise how defence policy and strategic deployment of crucial armed forces really drives us wild?

MP: I didn't know that. It's a shame that I'm not on the defence committee. Would talk about agriculture and fisheries do? I know a lot about that...

WOMAN: Oh...forget it! Handcuff me! Handcuff me!

MP: Hang on, who's that over there?

WOMAN: He's the local vicar. I suggested a threesome to him earlier...

MP: What?

VICAR: Hello. Do you like edible underwear?

DIVERTING EXCESS SEXUAL URGES INTO MORE HEALTHY AREAS

Look, I'm a red-blooded male MP who spends nearly all his time in a predominantly all-male environment. I've got natural urges (and a few unnatural ones too), how do you suggest I relieve my surplus sexual impulses (apart from the usual method)?

What do you mean, the 'usual method'?

You know, 'to Massage your Mace'...

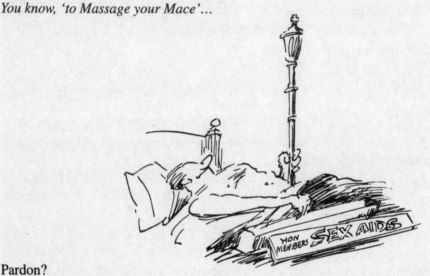

Pardon?

'To Whack off the Woolsack'.

I don't think I quite understand...

'To Flog your Finance Bill', 'Bang Big Ben', 'Pound your Petition'?

Er...We seem to have become diverted but let me now answer your original question. The Party recognises that some of its Members cannot control their sexual urges and it might be better to find a vent for these frustrations rather than have them build up and be released in some unhealthy manner.

What would you say was an 'unhealthy manner'?

Anything whatsoever involving a noose, ladies' stockings and an orange.

When you say ladies' stockings, what type do you mean?

White ones, 30 or 40 denier...Listen. That's irrelevant. As I was saying, one of the ways which MPs do vent their pent-up sexual urges – and I must point out that in no way does the Party actually condone this behaviour – is prostitution.

Pardon?

Prostitution.

Sorry?

Prostitution!!!

Oh yes. But what advice can you give me?

How about, 'Don't get caught'.

I meant apart from that.

Well, if you follow that suggestion it doesn't really matter who you sleep with.

So you're saying that it's OK to sleep with a prostitute?

No I am not!

Well, were you saying it's OK to wear women's stockings then?

No I bloody well wasn't!

OK. OK. But say I do sleep with a prostitute, is it easy to avoid detection?

Quite easy – however, be on your guard. There are certain little signs that you've been with one.

Like what?

I knew you were going to ask that...

Signs you've been with a prostitute:

*   You find your photo splashed all over the front page of the *News Of The World*.
*   You have a quizzical grin on your face (it's the first time you've been with a three-input woman).
*   When you wake up, you check on impulse to see if your wallet is still in your jacket pocket.
*   Your wife wonders why you leave £100 by the side of the bed when you leave the house in the morning.
*   Love bites in places where no normal woman would go near and it would be impossible to inflict upon yourself.
*   Shackle marks on your ankles and rope burns on your wrists.
*   An entry like '11.30 – Madame Bianca's Palais de Bonque' in your Parliamentary diary.
*   A huge bottle of antibiotics on your desk.

Where do I find these good women?

All I can divulge is that temptation lurks in every telephone kiosk around Westminster!

Beyond water sports! Let me show you my early day motion!

Tina:

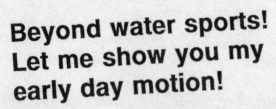

 Life Peer of long standing with own vaseline promises an easy passage through the Lords

I'm Thrusty, Your Big Ben Division and *Lusty and Busty! Put between my Commons lose your deposit!*

Delicious Dusky Dominatrix with own Black Rod Seeks Naughty MP to be de-selected

I'm
lobbying
for a
nobbying!
Errol:

Japanese Hand Maiden Is Waiting To Elect You...

My Hot Ballot Box Is Waiting for Your Vote (Don't waste it)

Say, for whatever reason, I did get caught, what could I do?

The first thing is to deny everything. You've got to have a convincing excuse. Try one of the following – they've worked for someone I know.

Excuses to make if you're accused of soliciting a prostitute:

* She's one of my constituents and I was just canvassing her.
* I was doing some research into self-employment and was just asking a few questions.
* I was set up by a Sunday newspaper. I've never seen Erica – or whatever her name was – before.
* I mistook her for one of my Parliamentary colleagues – Nigel (it was dark and they both wear the same leather hot pants).
* I was trying to persuade her to leave her life of vice and become my Commons researcher.
* There I was, innocently going about my own business at three o'clock in the morning at King's Cross when this brazen trollop solicited *me...*

*If accused of soliciting a prostitute claim you
were researching self-employment*

But what if the police catch me in my car, driving at 3 mph through King's Cross in the early hours of the morning?

In cases like this, you have to be much more inventive with your excuses:

Use these excuses when stopped by the police for kerb-crawling:

* I'm on the Commons Select Committee for Transport and I was just demonstrating one method of conserving fuel
* I was trying to avoid getting stopped for speeding
* Well, the ex-DPP did it and if it's good enough for him...
* I was practising my slow-driving technique including clutch control
* If you had a car as flashy as mine you'd want to show it off too by driving everywhere really slowly

Oh. What if I don't really want even to risk being caught. Is there a better way to ease my sexual frustrations?

Of course. Do what the majority of Tory MPs do.

What, you mean 'Massaging the Mace'?

No, apart from that. Are you married?

Yes.

Well, to get rid off your excess sexual urges, what about having sex with your wife?

You know, I never thought of that...

Well there you go.

Do you think she'll mind if I wear her stockings?

Go away...

Can I just ask one more thing?

No.

What about rent boys?

UNACCEPTABLE
BEHAVIOUR

EXTRA-MARITAL AFFAIRS

Here we go. I can see you're going to get all self-righteous with me over this subject.

Well of course! What do you expect me to say, 'If you're a married MP it's all right to shag as many women as you like'. Or, 'John Major doesn't care one single bit, in fact he's only going to appoint Cabinet members who have made it a habit of sleeping around?'

I thought that was current policy anyway...

Very funny. Listen, fidelity is the cornerstone of the PM's Back to Basics policy, but you degenerates seem to think that unless you have an affair you're not a *bona fide* representative of the Conservative Party.

But we can't help ourselves. Look, you're an MP too. You know us and our wives and, let's face it, not many of them are 'goers' are they?

I know, but...

I know for a fact your wife isn't...

What?

Come on, how many of our wives are adventurous in bed? They're only interested in one position – Number 10. It's not surprising we have to look elsewhere for what our illustrious leader would call 'rumpy pumpy'.

Listen, John Major knows the desire to have an affair is a genetic thing, locked deep within the male DNA code and there's nothing he can do to stop it.

So he's saying it is *all right to have an affair?*

He's saying nothing of the sort. What John Major is saying is that if, for some reason, you feel you've just got to have an affair, make sure it's with the right sort of person.

You mean someone that goes like a bloody train?

No. I mean someone who's discreet and loyal, with no interest whatsoever in blackmailing you or selling their story to the national press.

So what advice can you give me about having an affair?

Memorise the list overleaf before you do something you'll regret.

Like what? Like having sex with a large goose in public. Or trying to squeeze an entire honeydew melon up my bottom?

Pardon?

You said I should read the list before I do something I'll regret – I'd regret doing those. I think.

Look. Just read the list...

Suitable people to have an affair with (if you really, really can't help yourself):

* Anyone partially sighted
* Anyone that's got a terrible memory for faces
* A loyal Party member
* Anyone that's staying in this country on a dodgy visa and who could be deported at the drop of a hat in the dead of night
* That's about it, really

Completely unsuitable people to have an affair with:

* Norma Major
* The Queen
* Your mum
* The Queen Mum
* Your daughter
* Anyone working for a national newspaper
* Anyone working for a foreign government
* Any other Conservative MP
* Anyone dead
* Would-be actresses (see separate panel opposite)

One of the stable lads has got one this long.

The Queen Mum is a completely unsuitable person to have an affair with

IMPORTANT!!! SPECIAL ADVICE SECTION ON WOULD-BE ACTRESSES

Why have a separate section in the book devoted to the aspiring members of this fine profession?

Because they're gold-digging, two-faced, bed-hopping no-hopers out to be rich and famous for fifteen minutes while they ruin your career and humiliate the Party into the bargain.

But they're damn good lays.

So?

What other reason would you want? I mean, you don't go out with an actress so you can discuss Stanislavsky's Method-Acting Techniques, or for a critique of Pinter, do you?

No, I suppose not. Why would you want to go out with one of these women, knowing all the risks?

For a start, they can fake orgasms much more realistically.

Really?

Oh yes. They can really put on a convincing show so if you're a bit dodgy in bed, like if you have a really small todger – not that I have, of course – you don't feel so self-conscious about not being able to please.

I see. I presume that the same would apply if an MP suffered from, as an example, severe 'hair trigger' problems.

What, the type who you start leaking even when you're thinking of something fairly innocuous – like Edwina Currie in fisherman's waders?

Ohhhhhhhhhhh..........

Yes, that's it. Anyway, are there any other good reasons for dating an actress?

Well, because of their training they can take on virtually any role in the bedroom. Say your fantasy was being a slave master in Ancient Rome, then the actress could adapt to the role of submissive slave girl who'd do anything to win her freedom, even if it meant having to rub strawberry blancmange all over her body to the tune of the 'Birdie Dance'.

Interesting. So if someone had a fantasy, say, of dressing up as a naughty schoolboy whose punishment is to be given a coleslaw enema by his harsh governess, she could really get into the part?

I would think so.

Would I have to bring my own coleslaw?

I'm not sure.

Do would-be actors behave the same?

Yes.

John Major says...

Warning! Affairs can be a tangled web of social diseases!

Once you enter into an affair you can get sucked into a bottomless pit of depravity. Yes you can! Now you may think that all you're doing is having carnal knowledge with one or two floozies, but indirectly you're getting intimate with a lot of people with questionable morals, most of them your Parliamentary colleagues! These MPs will know who they are – mainly because I've listed their names opposite. So there.

Rt Hon Member for Pondsley West	**SLEPT WITH**
Roxy Tarte (would-be actress)	**SLEPT WITH**
Rt Hon Member for Harrington Green	**SLEPT WITH**
Sally Mason (his bi-sexual secretary)	**SLEPT WITH**
Marilyn Ashforth (bi-sexual go-go dancer)	**SLEPT WITH**
Prince (her alsatian)	**SLEPT WITH**
Rt Hon Member for Dorchester	**SLEPT WITH**
Rt Hon Member for Stapleforth & Huntley	**SLEPT WITH**
Sophia LaBianca (wife of Spanish ambassador)	**SLEPT WITH**
Rt Hon Member for Croxley	**SLEPT WITH**
Roxy Tarte (would-be actress)	**SLEPT WITH**
Steve Thomson (her bi-sexual boyfriend)	**SLEPT WITH**
Rt Hon Member for North Torrington	**SLEPT WITH**
Linda Dubbins (some old slapper)	

SLEPT WITH

BEHAVING IN PUBLIC

This is the part of the job that I really enjoy; getting out there and meeting the voters.

Yes, but be warned. All it takes is a careless off-the-cuff remark that's reported in the local paper and you'll be fighting for your political career.

But there are ways of using public engagements to your advantage. I'm a strong believer that a picture's worth a thousand words...

Or a thousand pounds if it shows you in bed with two venture scouts and a French loaf.

Precisely. That's why I choose the public engagements which seem to offer the best photo opportunities.

That's a good move – just so long as you *do* realise what makes a good photo opportunity. This should give you the idea:

This is an unsuitable photo opportunity

Photo opportunities

Good	Bad
Opening an old people's home	Closing an old people's home
Kissing a baby	Snogging the baby's mother
Accepting a petition on behalf of all your constituents	Accepting a backhander from one of your constituents
Laying the cornerstone for a new hospital	Laying one of the nurses
Shaking hands with the PM	Kissing the PM
Soliciting the views of a group of local residents	Soliciting some old tart round the back of King's Cross station
Marching alongside British veterans at a D-Day remembrance service	Goosestepping alongside British veterans at a D-Day remembrance service
Wearing a smart suit, standing in front of the Houses of Parliament	Wearing a noose and ladies' stockings, lying on a table

That's pretty damn obvious, isn't it? Tell me something I don't know.
How about door-to-door canvassing. Do you know much about that?
A little...
Do you know the optimum time to call on one of your constituents?
That's obvious – about 9.30 in the morning.
9.30am? For goodness sake, why?
Well, you know, the kids are at school, the husband's at work and the wife has just stepped out of the shower, maybe with her towel clinging to the contours of her damp, glistening body as she opens the door.

Door-to-door canvassing is fraught with temptation

You *do* need advice.

She beckons you to come in and in moments is standing naked in front of you, pouting and beckoning you to follow her up the stairs.

Excuse me!

There she motions you towards the bed and in seconds is astride...

That's quite enough!

Sorry.

Just pay attention...

What should I wear, then?

Whatever you feel most comfortable in.

Women's clothing?

Not that.

How about the flayed skin of a dead political opponent draped round me like a cape.

Uh?

Only kidding. All right, what's a good opening line?

That's easy. Basically anything that includes an appropriate greeting followed by an indication of who you are and what you want. Stick to this safe, proven format and you can't go far wrong.

You mean something like...um...er...something like...erm...um...I know. 'Good morning, I'm your local MP and I've called round to see how you feel about the new motorway extension.'

Very good. I can see that those three years at Cambridge was time well spent.

Thank you. But if that's the sort of thing we MPs should be saying on the doorstep, what shouldn't we be saying?

I'm glad you asked me that because it leads on nicely to the next element in this section.

I know. I peeked!

Cheat!

Bad opening lines to use when going door-to-door canvassing:

* Is your husband out, babe?
* Is your wife out, hunky?
* Hello, I'm from the water board. There's a severe water shortage and you've got to have a bath with me. Right now.
* Bet you've never seen one as big as this before...
* Hello little boy. Would you like to see some puppies...?
* I'm here to collect money on behalf of my local Transvestite Self-Help Group.
* Bob a job, missus? You know, a good seeing-to, only 20p. Doing it doggie-fashion, 5p more. Come on luv! Be a sport.
* That Major! What a prat, eh?
* Can I interest you in a copy of the Watchtower?
* Can I interest you in male-to-male sodomy?

OK. Supposing I can't be arsed to go door-to-door canvassing. All that walking. All that ringing bells and having doors slammed in your face. Is there anything else I can do to meet the punters?

Yes. You could always drive around safe in your loudspeaker car.

Do MPs still use them?

Occasionally. If they're lazy like you.

Well, what advice can you give me on the subject?

Make sure your knob's in.

I usually do, but what's that got to do with it?

Everything. The important thing to remember is that when the knob's in, you're broadcasting through the speakers. When it's pulled out, you're not. It's quite simple.

But it's not a knob that turns the speakers on or off, it's a switch.

Same difference.

No it's not. You just used the word 'knob' a few lines up to make some really childish smutty joke.

No I didn't. Anyway, as I was saying, the biggest blunder you can make using a loudspeaker car is to be talking, unaware that everything you say is being broadcast.

But only a prize chump would do that sort of thing.

Precisely. This is how the Rt Hon Member for Evesham North lost his 18,700 majority in the 1987 election. The following is a transcript from his final broadcast in the town centre on the day before the election:

...so for local prosperity and a town we can all be proud of, I ask you all to vote Tory tomorrow. Thank you...

It's good of you to drive me around Miss Brown but I really don't know why I bother with these stupid public appearances. With the majority I've got, it's a complete waste of time. The voters are like sheep – worse than sheep in fact; at least sheep have brains! And pert buttocks! The people here have voted for me in the last three elections and they'll do the same this time – you wait and see. Westminster here I come!

Do you know Miss Brown, that a day in London is more exciting than a year in this shitty old town. The best thing that could happen to it is if the nuclear waste reprocessing plant exploded and took everything with it. Oh…I forgot. Listen, that new plant's not going to be announced for another six months, so it's just between you and me, all right? Anyway, I'm so glad I'm not here during the week. Just the thought of returning to this provincial sewer and that ugly old sow I call a wife really depresses me. Still. Got to keep up appearances haven't you. And speaking of appearances you look delectable this morning, Miss Brown. Are you wearing those crotchless silk tights I bought you? Let me have a look. Come on…and is that your black silk basque I can detect under your jumper…the one with the Swastika on that I like you wearing…Come on. You can drive at the same time…Just let me put my hand up…Oh my God. The switch is on! Vote for me! Vote for Labour! Yes, I'm the local Labour candidate! Yes I am! And I've done it with your wives! All of them…

Crikey! This whole business of getting out there and meeting the punters is fraught with difficulty. I think I'm better off just holding my weekly surgery.

I think you're right. At least you can get to meet constituents on a regular basis.

That's right. What's more, it's a hell of a lot more fun.

Fun?

Yes, you know! When the girls strip down to their underwear and you can touch them up.

Pardon?

And the men. You can while away a pleasant hour or two poking about with the Marigolds, looking for the old prostate, if you're that way inclined.

What on earth are you talking about?

And my secretary. When she puts on those stockings and the nurse's uniform.

Oh!

Have we suddenly changed subjects?

No. We were talking about my weekly surgeries.

I should have guessed.

You look a bit peaky at the moment. I could treat you privately, you know. Cough please…

Special advice when kissing babies:
NO TONGUES!

THE ANNUAL PARTY CONFERENCE

The annual Conservative Party Conference is one of the highlights of our political year...

I'll say!!

Here we meet to form and debate policy, consult with rank and file members...

Rank and vile members, we call them. Jumped-up plebs!

...listen to keynote speeches by ministers...

Get drunk and run around the hotel trying to bonk anything you come across...

That, in a nutshell, is the problem. Too many MPs, like yourself, see the annual Party Conference as one long orgy – an excuse for several days of debauchery, drunkenness and perversion.

Yes. Wonderful, isn't it!

No. It must stop. Your behaviour at Party Conferences must exemplify Conservative Party values.

It does.

Values as defined by Back to Basics. Moderation, respectable behaviour...

I wouldn't bother going.

We understand the problem – the passions stirred after groundbreaking speeches by expert orators, the heady aphrodisiac of power being expertly wielded, the excitement of the cut and thrust of vigorous debate...

Drunk Commons researchers just gagging for it...

Look, Mr Major has said that – if this sort of behaviour continues – he will scrap the next Party Conference altogether.

Just because he goes to bed at 10.30 with a mug of cocoa...

He has received a strong letter of complaint from last year's venue and is intent on acting upon it. When you read this letter, reproduced overleaf, I am sure you will understand his position...

Hotel Continental
227 Southern Esplanade, Brighton, Sussex
★★★★★

Dear Mr Major,

While we welcome your custom and that of your Party – and we are honoured that the Conservatives have chosen this hotel in which to base themselves during their annual conference – we feel that we can 'suffer in silence' no longer.

A number of members of our staff are extremely upset about the behaviour of members of your party at the conference and are refusing to do their jobs on days when you are in residence.

We think you will agree when you peruse these sample complaints logged by the hotel on just one night during your last conference:

23.07   'Indecent Proposal' scenario in lobby as MP offers a guest 50p to sleep with his wife.

23.08   Guest declines offer to sleep with MP's wife.

23.10   MP dives out of fourth floor window into outdoor swimming pool [this is a practice we particularly discourage, as we do not have an outdoor swimming pool].

23.11   Complaint received from Brighton Petting Zoo re: missing animals

23.12   Noise complaint received – from Mrs M. Davisdon of Blackpool.

23.13   Concierge offered £100 to 'come upstairs and party'.

23.13   Goat found wandering on seventh floor.

23.15   Concierge told that there's been a whip round and they can now offer him £150 to come upstairs.

23.15   Mini-bar hurled into street from 10th floor narrowly missing police guard.

23.16   Prominent member of Cabinet reported drinking heavily in bar, stark naked apart from sock over his private parts.

23.17   Fight starts in bar as well known Tory Euro rebel attempts to reclaim his sock from prominent member of cabinet.

23.18   Prominent member of Cabinet, now with streaming nose bleed, reported to be upsetting drinkers in the bar by doing impressions of **Tony Blair with his private parts.**

23.19   Guests leave bar as another prominent member of the Cabinet does his impersonation of Tony Blair being swallowed by a whale...

23.20   Hotel security arrive to be told by second Cabinet member that he is doing nothing more than enjoying a quiet drink...He is advised to leave the bar.

23.21   Hotel security invited upstairs to 'sort us out properly'.

23.22   Guest complains of 'chicken in distress' noises coming from floor above.

23.23   Ambulance called after backbencher accidentally sets off fire extinguisher while sitting on it in the nude.

23.24   Concierge now offered £175.50 – provided he will let individuals concerned call him 'Juicy Jason' for course of evening. He declines

23.27	Room Service is requested to deliver four boys of Arab extraction and 300 jars of Robinson's Marmalade to tenth floor. They regret that they cannot comply.
23.37	Fire hose reported stolen from tenth floor.
23.38	Second ambulance called after MP accidentally tangles himself up in TV extension cord after stripping for bed and then tripping over and accidentally sitting down on a large brass bed knob.
23.41	Hotel Security called to break up impromptu game of 'naked kiss chase' on tenth floor.
23.43	MP in French Maid's outfit found drunk and unconscious in lift
23.45	Rock group Guns N' Roses leave hotel after complaining about the persistent noise and bad behaviour.
23.47	Room service despatched to 10th floor with tweezers as requested. Fail to remove champagne cork from backbencher's anus.
23.48	Member of room service staff walks out in disgust.
23.49	Member of room service staff returns, complaining that he has been vomited upon from a tenth floor balcony whilst leaving.
23.50	Hotel security find wombat in lift wearing red garter belt. Brighton Petting Zoo informed.
00.02	Tug of war ensues in hotel lobby over wombat between staff of Brighton Petting Zoo and sobbing MP with bocquet of flowers referring to said wombat as 'darling Boo-Boo'
00.03	Female commons researcher runs shrieking through lobby.
00.04	Male Party agent runs shrieking through lobby, brandishing large unidentified vibrating object.
00.07	Request for room service to deliver 400 feet of mains cable and a bag of Jaffas to tenth floor vetoed by hotel security.
00.07	Vacuum cleaner reported stolen from storeroom on seventh floor.
00.12	Third ambulance called after party activist accidentally sits down upon large cacti while nude. Drink suspected.
00.13	Female commons researcher runs shrieking through lobby again.
00.14	Male Party agent runs shrieking through lobby again, brandishing large unidentified vibrating object and jar of Hellman's mayonnaise
00.15	Plaster cast of unidentified penis found in lift.
00.15	Bed thrown from tenth floor window.
00.17	Fire brigade called to free well-known backbencher dangling from balcony with rope around his genitals. Clearly worse for drink, he tells rescue services he was trying 'bollock-bunjee jumping'.

These events represent less than two hours out of a total of three consecutive days.

We are sure then that you will realise the gravity of the situation and act accordingly to prevent this frankly disgraceful state of affairs from occuring again this year.

Thanking you in advance for your co-operation in these matters.

Yours sincerely,

Geoff Davies

Manager

NEW YEAR'S HONOURS

So the PM's going to continue with his policy of widening access to the New Year's Honours?

That's right, I'm afraid to say.

Why? I thought the Whip's Office was supposed to be supportive of Johnnie Boy.

We are, except that a policy like this is open to abuse from backbenchers.

What do you mean?

You know very well what I'm talking about. Last year when the PM set up his Honours Committee he was inundated with nominations from the public for people they thought were deserving of an award.

So what's wrong with that?

Among the nominations were 714 for an OBE for a certain 'Miss Whiplash' – all of which were received in the House of Commons internal post. The other nominations shown here are typical of those received from his own MPs.

So?

Well Mr Major wants people nominated for their services to the public – not personal services.

Really? Let me tell you that Miss Whiplash is just as valid a choice as some old biddy who's worked for Meals on Wheels for thirty years.

So you think you can compare Miss Whiplash with a voluntary worker, do you?

Yes. She works extremely hard behind the scenes and thousands of people are very glad to see her.

But she doesn't help the sad, lonely and aged, does she?

No? Why don't you talk to the House of Lords?

Point taken.

A selection of New Year's Honours forms reviewed and subsequently rejected by Mr Major

New Year's Honours - Nomination Form

Name ▓▓▓▓ Address Hause d Commons,
Person nominated Dominatrix Dawn
Reason for nomination 46-28-32!

New Year's Honours - Nomination Form

Name ▓▓▓▓ Address House of Commons, London
Person nominated P.C. Jeff Markham + Colleagues
Reason for nomination For turning a blind eye
that night he raided the 'CAFÉ DONG' club
in Soho - you know, the one that features
that donkey act.

New Year's Honours - Nomination Form

Name ▓▓▓▓ Address HOUSE OF COMMONS
Person nominated JULIAN CLARY
Reason for nomination
HE'S SO SCRUMMY!

New Year's Honours - Nomination Form

Name ▓▓▓▓ Address HOUSE OF COMMONS,
LONDON
Person nominated LORD CHIEF JUSTICE ROYSTON
(MY CHUBBY BUNNY)
Reason for nomination
HE KNOWS...

New Year's Honours - Nomination Form

Name ▓▓▓▓ Address Hause d Commons
Person nominated Fred Williams, Fruiterers
Reason for nomination They have the
longest, firmest courgettes I have
ever tried!

John Major says...

Sometimes, when I'm having my sandwiches at Number 10 (not to forget my Cadbury's mini-roll and bag of Mini-Cheddars which Norma so kindly packs for me in my Transformers lunchbox), I think who I'd award honours to if I could choose anyone in the entire world.

Of course, in real life I always consult with the Honours Committee because not doing so would undermine democracy, oh my word yes. These are the sort of people I'd reward for their services if it were left solely to me:

- The man who invented Chocolate Hob Nobs
- Matthew Corbett (the maestro himself)
- Glenn Hoddle (my hero)
- Richard Digence (what catchy tunes)
- Jane Torville (better not show Norma this list. She might become a little too jealous!!!)
- Christopher Biggins (a fine actor if ever there was one)
- Bernie Clifton (his act always manages to surprise me)
- Bobby Davro (Mr Comedy)
- John Craven (why can't all journalists behave as professionally as he does?)
- Philip Schofield and Emma Forbes (such a lovely couple. I hope they get married)
- Tony Monopoly (come back, wherever you are!)
- Mary Nightingale (a gorgeous newscaster who makes even the bad news sound good)

ADVERTISING AND PRODUCT ENDORSEMENTS

Appearing in advertisements and endorsing products has, over the years, proved a very lucrative source of income for Members of Parliament from Clement Freud's endorsement of dog food – or is it Bird's Eye cuisine these days?

Same difference...

...to ex-Labour Chancellor Denis Healey advertising banking services.

From the offers Conservative MPs are presently receiving, however, it appears that we are largely considered as figures of fun. The ideas our MPs are being approached with depict us as a bunch of perverts – quite the opposite of what Back to Basics is intended to achieve.

For this reason, MPs must submit all potential advertising offers to Central Office for vetting.

Here are some we have rejected recently. I think you will appreciate why...

Isn't it good to be in control?

You can in a Nissan

We can't believe it's not butter

The choice for a new generation

1

- 71 -

BEING EXPOSED

THE MEDIA AND YOU

In the real world, our relationship with the media is – at best – a double-edged sword. We need it to get our policies across to the electorate – and they want to land us in it at every opportunity.

At the moment, the BBC in particular is very keen to catch us out over alleged hypocrisy with Back to Basics. They will start off on a fairly innocuous topic and then suddenly turn up the heat on a vulnerable issue.

If you find yourself live on television, and the pressure is on, follow this sensible advice:

These are suitable phrases to get you out of trouble:

* Yes, but under the last Labour Government...
* I don't think that's a fair question...
* That's just the sort of biased line of questioning we've come to expect from the BBC at present...
* I'm sure you'd agree that journalists are not exactly paragons of virtue either...
* I object to this frankly impertinent line of questioning...
* But to return to Labour Party policy...
* I'm sorry; I can't hear you. We seem to be experiencing some technical difficulties at this end...
* I have every confidence in Mr Major's leadership.

These are *not* suitable phrases:

* It takes one to know one!
* Shut up, you pompous gobshite!
* Let he who is without sin cast the first stone – and I know where your rocks are most evenings, duckie...
* I know...but I'm not telling!
* I'll punch you in a minute.
* I'm going to put my hands over my ears and refuse to listen.
* You caught me out. We're guilty as charged, I'm afraid.
* Yes, we should have a leadership contest.

I don't mind the BBC so much; it's the tabloids who terrify me.
And quite rightly. It doesn't matter you say to them, they'll twist it around and distort it somehow.

For example, you say, 'The question of European federalism and its relation to national sovereignty is under further discussion'.

They print, ' "HOP OFF YOU FROGS," SAY TORIES!'.

You say, 'In order to maximise job opportunities, workers must be prepared to relocate to areas where their skills are in demand'.

They print, ' "TORIES TELL UNEMPLOYED: ON YER BIKE!"'.'

And those are examples of better reporting. Other accounts given by Tory MPs may be subject to even greater distortion.

For example, you say, 'Changing indirect taxation will have a profound effect on our domestic fiscal situation'.

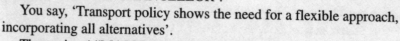

They print, ' "I'VE DONE IT WITH GOATS," CLAIMS CHANCELLOR'.

You say, 'Transport policy shows the need for a flexible approach, incorporating all alternatives'.

They print, ' "MAJOR MUST GO," DEMANDS BACKBENCHER.

You say, 'Major must go.'

They print, ' "BACKBENCHER MUST GO," SAYS MAJOR'.

We will be urgently reviewing the power of the press in the next Parliament.

Surely this doesn't apply to the good old 'Thunderer'. Surely The Times *can still be trusted to give us fair coverage and act as a decent platform for Conservative MPs to express their views...*

Certainly. The Letter Column, for example, still remains a bastion of Tory values. However, we are most concerned about the sad decline in the quality of letters being sent to the column by Conservative MPs recently. With the kind permission of *The Times*, a few examples are reprinted opposite:

Sir,

Wot a load of rubish the labor party are speaking about the educashonal debate wot is going on at present. Grammar wot is good is wot we will always stand for in our party coz a good educashon means lots and not this poncy soshal science and homo lessons and Lezzies in the clasroom like wot the labor party wants.

Toby McCabe-Richards, MP Chelsea North.

Sir,

I am worried that I am falling in love with my sister-in-law. Like me, she is married with two children and neither of us want to break up our families but I feel there is a strong attraction between us. Should I tell her how I feel?

'Worried', Westminster

The Editor replies: *For the sake of both your families, it would be best to say nothing. This is just an infatuation and will pass if neither of you does anything to encourage it.*

Sir,

Three cheers for *Emmerdale Farm*! The acting, dialogue and filming are all first rate!

Sir Adrian DeCourcey MP Brighton Central

Sir,

Can you settle a bet for me? I say England have only reached the World Cup final once, in 1966, but the Right Honourable Member for Salisbury West says they have reached the final twice. Can you tell me who is right? We have ten shillings on this.

James McBride, MP Canterbury South East

The Editor replies: *You are, sir! I hope you enjoy spending your ten bob!*

Sir,

Can you please print a picture of Catherine Zeta Jones [preferably a full frontal shot] as I think she is one of the most beautiful and talented young actresses on our screens.

Dinsdale Langdon-Pratt, MP Twickenham North East

The Editor replies: *Certainly not!*

Sir,

Before the last election, my five-year-old grandson said to me, 'Are you standing for Parliament, grandad'. When I told him I was, he asked, 'Well, how come you're sitting down then?' How we laughed! Do I win £5?

Oswald Mosley-Snetterton, QC, MP Slough and District

The Editor replies: *No.*

If we cannot improve upon this level of political debate, we should refrain from writing letters to *The Times* altogether.

It's a waste of time anyway. They didn't publish my limerick.

Oh God.

And it took me hours to think up a rhyme for 'vagina'.

LOVE CHILDREN
AKA 'DOING A TIM'
AKA 'DOING A CECIL'

The one phrase every MP dreads hearing from his mistress is…
'Eeuhhh! No! That's so gross! I'm not going to do that for you…'
I…
'When they said you had a slender majority, they were right!'
Listen…
'I can't go on living this dreadful lie! I am not going to dress up as a woman every time we go out in public…and you can call me Alan from now on. This "Tina" nonsense has got to stop.'
The phrase every *normal* MP dreads hearing from his mistress is – 'I'm pregnant'.

I suppose that's a pretty terrible thing to hear – but not as terrible as 'Now I've got you handcuffed to the bed, I can do anything I like to you. Where did I put that egg whisk?' In fact, finding out your mistress is pregnant by you is a doddle...

A doddle, is it?

Oh yeah, bung her a few hundred quid to make all the necessary arrangements with the clinic, send her a cheap Marks and Spars potted plant and tell the dozy cow you really love her. Problem over.

Supposing she wants to keep the child?

I see what you mean. That's a bit of a Michael Heseltine, isn't it?

What? A bastard?

No, a poser.

Yes. It's certainly a difficult moral dilemma. How will your wife feel about it? Or your constituency Party agent?

I don't know about my wife, but my local Party agent will probably go off in a big sulk and refuse to sleep with me ever again.

There is nothing the public like more than the spectacle of an MP fathering a love child. And that doesn't begin to cover the question of maintenance...

It is a frightening thought, isn't it? Perhaps we should shut down the CSA, stop them hounding all those poor innocent fathers for crippling maintenance payments! It's a national scandal! A disgrace! I shall raise it in the House!

Love children are at the very heart of Back to Basics. They are unacceptable proof of an MP's infidelity and untrustworthiness. We cannot afford to have any more scandals of this nature in the Party.

The Prime Minister has put forward several suggestions – including compulsory vasectomies and mass castration – but he was very cross at the time over this Tim Yeo business and the fact that he'd just bought a new packet of Mint Imperials and left them behind at the counter.

The simple solution, of course, is not to have sex.

No. The really simple solution is only to have gay sex. Quite a nice one, really. I'd settle for that, if I had to. It'd be like being back at school in the dorms...

That is not an acceptable solution. Gay sex is frowned upon just as much as straight sex in our Back to Basics policy.

Well, what am I supposed to do to contain my steaming libido, inflamed by the heady aphrodisiac of the power an MP knows he wields?

Masturbate.

What?

It works for the Lib-Dems; it can work for us too...

No! Look, if I wanted my sex life to be comprised exclusively of masturbation, I'd have stayed a chartered accountant instead of running for office.

John Major says...

I'm sorry. This has gone quite far enough. I cannot condone - and indeed the Party must not condone - acts of an unnatural nature.

Apart from which, I have to shake hands with these people on a regular basis.

I know that serving in Parliament can be a lonely business sometimes. Goodness, how I know it. The feeling that no-one likes you, that they're all talking about you behind your back, the sense of isolation you feel even within the bosom of your own Party. It's enough to make a grown man cry sometimes. Bastards!

I take solace from the love and support of my own family. They are all I need. Sometimes, if the stress and the loneliness get on top of me, I console myself with a biscuit. Or two. Or even an entire packet.

What I am saying is, you should not seek diversion from the stresses of Parliamentary life in shallow and tawdry sexual liaisons.

I am a man of the world and a father. I understand that it is hard to live up to the high standards we set ourselves and that sometimes, inevitably, one or two of us may slip from the path of the straight and narrow. Tim, for one. Or Cecil. I cannot stop you from having affairs, but I would be remiss in my duty as leader of this Party if I did not offer you some advice.

You may not be aware of this, but – if you are privy to the right procedure – you can get more from a gentleman's barber than a haircut. If you were to wink at him and say 'something for the weekend, I think, Mr. Barber', he will discreetly slip you a mysterious little packet which you would do well to take. Something which will help you to avoid unwanted pregnancies occurring. Of course, these items can be used at times other than weekends – that is just a euphemism used in the secret exchange – but can be relied upon on any day of the week.

Do not ask me how I know this. Just follow my advice to the letter and all will become clear.

I am not condoning extra-marital liaisons, you understand, but offer this advice to MPs who cannot follow our strict Back to Basics policy in the hope that they will at least avoid fatherhood out of wedlock.

Sound words of advice there from our leader.

Personally, I think denial's the answer.

Good! You mean not allowing yourself to have sex at all.

No. Denying you're the father.

DIARIES AND MEMOIRS

What's the Party policy on publishing diaries or memoirs?

It's a jolly good idea – a way of increasing your political profile as well as a truly excellent means of supplementing your income (though not as good as having a national newspaper print some story about you seeing a prostitute and you suing them for hundreds of thousands of pounds).

So you'd have no objection if I had a go?

What, at suing a national newspaper?

No. At my diaries. I'm thinking of publishing my political diaries. Would there be any problem?

Well, no – providing that it represented your time in politics in a fair and factual way and didn't have some tacky title or cover that brought you and the Party into disrepute.

Yes, but if you can't rely on your name alone to sell biographies, like Maggie or Alan Clark, you've got to have a good title that makes it leap off the bookshelves.

Are you suggesting that you're going to rely on some lewd, salacious title to make the bestsellers list? Because if you are, think again. The Party's in enough trouble over Back to Basics without you aggravating the problem.

If you want an idea of the sort of titles we do and do not want for diaries and memoirs just look at the following list:

These are approved titles for MPs' diaries or memoirs:

In the Corridors Of Power
To Serve The People
The Politics Of Compromise
Ever The Diplomat
Constitutional Guardian
A Maverick At Westminster

These are definitely not:

Humping In The House
Confessions Of A Bonking Backbencher
Shackled Sex Vixens Of Smith Square
General Election Gang Bang
Question Time Queens
Bi-Elected!
Select Committee Sex Sluts
Rampant Shag Frenzy! My Four Years On The Backbenches
Shaven Ombudsman Orgy
Life Peer or Pervert?
A Referendum Of Rogering
My Sexual Fantasies About Lady Thatcher
My Sexual Fantasies About Douglas Hurd
My Sexual Fantasies About Lady Thatcher and Douglas Hurd At It

OK, so I'll choose a nice, safe, boring title so it will probably sell 263 copies. Happy now? Should I edit the diaries and then approach a publisher or do it the other way round?

Neither. Before you do anything you should show them to John Major.

I can't do that! I've referred to him as 'that word' – on probably every page, and certainly in the title...

Don't be difficult. Suppose you've been complimentary to the Prime Minister, he will still want to look over your manuscript.

So he can write a really nice introduction?

No, so he can approve it.

Don't you mean 'censor it'?

Well, he's got the interests of the Party at heart, especially after the trouble we had last year with *A Commoner In The House* (formerly *Hot Scrotal Lust Action In The Lobby*) by the Rt Hon Member for Westerton.

Fortunately, the PM saw a copy of the manuscript before it went to the publishers – and just in the nick of time. There would have been hell to pay if it had been printed as intended. The following extract is typical of the rewrites that John ordered (I think you can see why...):

Before:
When it came down to it, the plebs in the street believed that totally false story I leaked to the press about the Labour Cabinet all giving Michael Foot's dog a good rogering.

Of course, we were gobsmacked when Maggie stayed in No.10 for 11 years. Mind you, I was well-chuffed to be by her side and tried to get off with her constantly 'cos I didn't reckon her husband was giving her enough. The stupid bitch played hard to get, even though I was the best-endowed bloke in the Cabinet and I could get unlimited drugs from my contacts at Customs & Excise.

After:
When it came to voting, the public remembered all-too-well the failures of the incumbent Labour Government and were ready to embrace a new administration.

Of course, we were all totally unprepared for the extent of Mrs Thatcher's term in office and dominance in politics for the next ten years. I was proud to play an important role in her Cabinet during her first term, not least because out of it developed a close personal relationship and respect and admiration for her leadership qualities.

I prefer the original version.
I thought you would.
I don't blame him trying to get off with Maggie. What a hot number she was! All that power. That strength. That brute aggression. That tight blue suit. Mistress Maggie, that's what we used to call her.
I'm sure you did, but remember that Mr Major is now at the helm.
I don't fancy him. Look, to save me wasting my time having to rewrite it, can you give me some guidance as to what's acceptable in my own memoirs.
Tell me what sort of subjects you were going to cover in this *Magnum Opus.*
Are you being sarcastic?
Whatever gave you that idea?

Good. I thought I'd begin by telling everyone that my local Young Conservatives Association was 'pussy heaven'.

I don't think so, somehow...

OK, then there'll be a bit about how I became a local Party worker by getting my leg over our MP's agent.

No there won't...

I'll devote a chapter to how I slept with our MP's wife, got her to leave her husband and then dumped her.

Carry on. I can see this is going to be quite a thin book...

I thought I'd continue with how I got our MP de-selected by implicating him in a county-wide animal-sodomy ring.

I think we're talking pamphlets here...

Your involvement in an animal-sodomy ring is not the sort of material we would expect in an autobiography

A bit about how I got to be the prospective Parliamentary candidate by setting up all my rivals with Thai rent boys and blackmailing them.

Or even two a two-sided A4 leaflet...

Then a chapter on how I shagged the returning officer senseless at my first by-election to make sure I'd win.

You can't write that...

A few pages on all the backhanders I've accepted from businessmen – names, dates and amounts, that sort of thing.

Or that!

Quite a bit about my sexual conquests in the Commons and how it was me that introduced that new strain of syphilis that ran riot through the backbenches a couple of years ago.

Stop it!

Ending up with a few pages on how I'd worked my way up the Conservative Party ladder by offering my body to three present Cabinet members.

I see. Tell me, did you have a title for this book.

I did, but it was a bit sensational. I'm going to follow your advice and tone it down to something much more suitable.

And that is?

'The Honourable Member'.

PARLIAMENTARY PRIVILEGE

Parliamentary Privilege is just that – a privilege. It should not be used just as a convenient way of making wildly slanderous accusations against fellow MPs without fear of legal consequences. The media can use anything you say and what may just start off as a casual insult against a fellow backbencher may become a full-blown scandal and cause our Back to Basics policy no end of harm.

Sorry. I was just scratching my rash... What did you say?

You do know what 'Parliamentary Privilege' is, don't you?

Of course, I'm an MP, aren't I?

Well yes – but some of your colleagues might not know – or they might have forgotten. I think I'd better explain it for everyone.

Apart from excusing them from serving on juries or attending courts as witnesses, Parliamentary Privilege gives MPs exemption from being sued for slander or libel over anything said during Parliamentary proceedings or published in its order paper.

I know. It's brilliant isn't it?

What do you mean?

It's great. If you want, you can shout across the chamber to the Opposition 'the Rt Hon Member for Rushton South is into hardcore S & M bondage in a big way' – and there's nothing he can do about it.

Precisely the point I am trying to make. It doesn't really matter if the allegation about the Opposition MP isn't true (although I think it might well be in the case of the Rt Hon Member for Rushton South), rumours will start to spread anyway.

Next thing you know, the MP in question is all over the tabloids. Now this isn't so bad when it's a member of the Opposition – in fact we can all have a jolly good laugh about it. Where it does matter is when it's about us. Remember, it could just as easily be a Tory MP who's into hardcore S & M bondage.

Oh. Like who?

I can think of 128 names off the top of my head for a... Look. That's not the point. I was using it as an example. Whenever an MP abuses Parliamentary Privilege it all ends up in some almighty slanging match. You remember the last time this happened?

No.

That's convenient – I'll show you...

Claiming that a political opponent is a man trapped in a woman's body or that he married a goat is an abuse of Parliamentary Privilege

The last time Parliamentary Privilege was abused – as reported by Hansard.

Tuesday, 16 May 1985:

Rt Hon Member for Weston: Mr Speaker, I should like to point out that the balance of trade figures put forward by the Rt Hon Member for Wakehampstead contained several blatant inaccuracies.

Rt Hon Member for Wakehampstead: Mr Speaker, I would like to make the House aware that the Rt Hon Member for Weston was a stupid minor public school-educated oik who failed his Maths O-level because he was too busy playing with himself when he should have been revising and is therefore the last member in the House who should pass judgement on these figures.

Rt Hon Member for Bridlington: Mr Speaker, I would remind the House that the Rt Hon Member for Wakehampstead does it with marmalade-covered choirboys.

Rt Hon Member for Tees Valley: Mr Speaker, it pleases me to inform you that the Rt Hon Member for Bridlington screwed his dead mother for three days and is a registered heroin addict.

Rt Hon Member for Onnington: Mr Speaker, it should be pointed out that the Rt Hon Member for Bridlington also has scabies.

Rt Hon Member for Upper Minebury: Mr Speaker, it is common knowledge that the Rt Hon Members for Bridlington and Weston are lovers.

Rt Hon Member for Chigley Forest: Mr Speaker, I should like to express my endorsement of this accusation but would like to add that they both used to be women.

Rt Hon Member for Lawnley Heath: Mr Speaker, I must inform the House that the Rt Hon Member for Chigley Forest is currently concealing Lord Lucan in his London flat.

Rt Hon Member for Chigley Forest: Mr Speaker, I must denounce these accusations vehemently and at the same time state that the Rt Hon Member for Lawnley Heath is a Russian spy and, furthermore, eats babies.

[At this point the House erupted in uproar. Unable to keep order any longer, Mr Speaker suspended this session of Parliament.]

I see what you mean. I didn't realise it could get so out of control and incriminate everyone. Anyway, what's the punishment?

Apart from humiliation and exposure in the press, if an MP breaches Parliamentary Privilege the Speaker can suspend or expel him. Under old laws the Speaker is also empowered to imprison him.

Imprison him?

Yes. Lock him up beneath the Houses of Parliament.

What, chain him up and all that?

That sort of thing.

Sounds like the Rt Hon Member for Rushton South would enjoy it.

DAMAGE
LIMITATION

THE ART OF COVER-UPS

So, someone has taken compromising photographs of you and...
They have?
Wait...
Oh my God! My career's ruined! You were right. I should have followed Back to Basics. I should have led a decent, moral life! I'll resign, devote the rest of my life to good charitable works...or at least lay low until all the worst has blown over and then re-emerge in a Cabinet post like nothing happened! I'm so sorry...
Stop...
I bet it was that blowsy tart at the last Party Conference...
No...
The Toblerone incident...

Some incidents will require an immediate cover-up

Hold on...
It was those two beefy black workmen who came to sort out my plumbing in the flat, wasn't it! The camera wasn't on when the plunger...or that bit of 'S' bend...?

No...

Oh my God...Don't tell me it was the Andrex puppy...please!

Stop! Hold on! This is just a hypothetical device to introduce this section...

You bastard! You did that on purpose!

If truth be told [not something which goes on a lot around here], the answer is 'yes'. You see, now you know...

He does it with stoats!

I do not!

Stoats, weasels, upside down kitchen stools and Woolworths check-out girls!

I bloody well do not!

If you could see him, he's wearing a little black Coco Chanel *dress right now.*

I am not! I'm in a suit and tie! A blue tie!

...With a pearl necklace given to him by someone in the Cabinet. And you know what I mean by a 'pearl necklace'...

Be quiet! That's just the kind of Party in-fighting which damages us in the public eye! As I was saying, now you know what it feels like to be 'caught at it'. Terrifying, isn't it? You really should have lived by our Back to Basics code. But, if you can't, you must at least learn the art of 'covering up'.

As an MP you are exceptionally vulnerable to exposure and, therefore, to blackmail. If you have been unfortunate enough to allow yourself to become ensnared in a ruthless blackmail scheme, the solution may have to be quite...extreme.

The most drastic solution to the problem, of course, is to have your blackmailer killed.

When all that business blew up with ex-Liberal leader Jeremy Thorpe, he was falsely accused of hiring a hitman to sort out the problem. If you decide to follow the same route, at least try to employ one who shoots your blackmailer, not his dog...

Maybe the dog was a star witness...

I don't think so.

A canine supergrass...

Unlikely...

Maybe he got confused. They say dogs get to look like their owners. Maybe Norman Scott looked like his dog...

It doesn't matter why it happened.

Maybe the hitman was very shortsighted. God knows, the Liberals haven't

*got much money and probably couldn't afford a normal, healthy, halfway
decent hitman...*

Jeremy Thorpe did *not* hire a hitman. He was found not guilty at the Old
Bailey.

Oh. Right. I understand.

It's just an example...Now, if you were to find yourself being blackmailed
and decided upon this course of action, the most important thing to do is not
to implicate the Tory Party in your actions. That means no claiming for 'A
hitman' on your expenses, no asking Kenneth Baker if he'd do it as a favour
and no calling cards on the body saying 'You have been done up a treat by
the Tory Party boys' or 'So perish all those who attempt to blackmail
Conservative MPs'.

*Just suppose I...er...needed a hitman. Not that I'll ever need one, of course.
How would I go about finding one?*

Read on...

Hitmen

Good places to find them:

* East End pubs
* Down at the docks
* Through a 'friend of a friend'
* Through the small ads of *Soldier of Fortune* magazine
* Down a dark alleyway in Soho
* Coming out of the local Army recruitment office in a huff after being
turned down for being 'too mentally unstable'

Bad places to find them:

* Yellow Pages
* Dancing the male lead in *Swan Lake*
* Advertising in a 'situations vacant' column
* Serving twenty years to life in Pentonville
* On a Government training scheme
* In a Salvation Army band
* In your wardrobe, waiting for *you*...

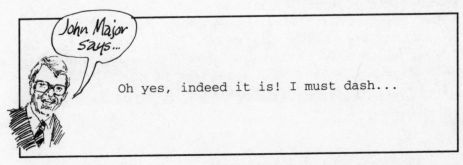

> **John Major says...**
>
> What's all this about hiring hitmen? It's most irregular and I am afraid I cannot condone it as a solution. There must be more civilised ways of conducting our affairs...

Wait, Prime Minister... Oh look, isn't that the Commons tea trolley doing its rounds? You'd better hurry and get in the queue before all the Jacobs Club Biscuits are gone. I hear there are orange ones today...

> **John Major says...**
>
> Oh yes, indeed it is! I must dash...

Phew! That got rid of him! All right, I think we've talked quite enough about...you know.

Of course, you may choose to pay your blackmailer to keep silent. Here, the Party can be of more help to you. We have over £1 million in a secret fund for just such a contingency...

Oh. I am being blackmailed after all. And what a coincidence! That's precisely the sum of money they're asking for! If you can have it ready in used tenners in a suitcase by four, I'll fly out to the Bahamas to meet them with it...

Liar.

It was worth a try...

Requests for blackmail money should be put through your expenses as 'ex-gratia staff payments' or 'Malaysian charity aid'. When you meet with your blackmailer, you should handle the situation professionally and firmly:

The right things to say to your blackmailer:

* That's all you're getting.
* Take it. Now, breathe a word of this to anyone and it's the last breath you'll take...
* Now we're even.
* This is not an admission of guilt; I just don't want any trouble...
* There's this Labour backbencher who's doing it with one of TV's *Gladiators*. Do you want to know more?

The wrong things to say to your blackmailer:

* You'll get not a penny from me! I'm not afraid of my political career being in tatters, my Party discredited, a long stretch in prison and possible private prosecution by the RSPCA! Do your worst!
* Here you go, and there's plenty more where that came from if you want to go on blackmailing me for the rest of my life.
* Would you like to take some more pics of me? I'm wearing suspendies under this suit...
* It's a good thing you didn't know about me and the Dulux dog.

If being blackmailed, don't admit to anything
more than you have to

This advice is all very well if I am being blackmailed by a private individual, but how do I arrange a cover-up if the press gets wind of the story and decides to publish?

John Major Says...

Bastards! I queued for the tea trolley for ages, and when I got to the front of the queue someone had bought all the Club biscuits.

It's a conspiracy - a conspiracy to hound me out of my position as leader of the Party! Well, it just won't work! I'll get Norma to put extra Jacobs Clubs in my Transformers lunch box in future! I'll bring them with me from home, you see if I don't! I have a programme to carry out, with a mandate from the people, and I won't abandon it and let down the electorate just because you bastards think it's funny to buy up my favourite biscuits every day before I can get to them! Bastards!

Er...sorry. Where were you?

We were just discussing how to effect a cover-up in the face of press disclosure, Prime Minister.

John Major Says...

Frankly, in a situation of this nature, I feel that the best course of action is not to engage in a cover-up which may have more damaging repercussions later, but to do the honourable thing and resign. People soon forget and you can then come back in and start where you left off...

Bastards! No one likes the ones with raisins in, except me! They probably don't even eat them. They probably go straight in the bin!

*I don't want to be besmirched! Smeared in yoghourt, yes. Tied up with flex
and have a rolled-up copy of* The Spectator *forced into my back passage and
used as a funnel to pour warm chocolate milk through, yes – but I refuse to
be besmirched by anyone!*

If the press does decide to publish, then your only course of action is to get a
court injunction against the newspapers and then take legal action against
them for spreading lies about you.

But what if it's the truth?

You remember what you were saying...about the rolled-up copy of *The
Spectator* and the warm chocolate milk?

Yes.

Who is it who does that for you on Thursday nights?

Oh. What's his name? Judge...

Right.

Oh, right. I understand.

Good.

Isn't British justice wonderful?

THE SUPPORT OF YOUR FAMILY

When a scandal breaks, the most valuable thing you can have is the support of your family.

I would have thought a decent alibi would be preferable.

Apart from that. If your wife is seen to stand by you and declare her love and support for you, the public think you can't be that bad a person after all. If your wife can forgive you, then they will too.

Now let's put ourselves in an imaginary position where your wife has found out about an affair you've been having. The very first thing you must do is ensure you do not make matters any worse than they already are. Say something kind and conciliatory, rather than taking a defiant stance.

When she challenges you about sleeping with another woman, *don't* say:

* Several women, actually!
* Mind your own business, bitch!
* It took you long enough to work that out!
* I still love you; she's only there for the sex
* Hey! Have I still got it or what!
* That's such a crazy idea, I'm going to have you committed forthwith
* She had great tits; what can I say?
* What are you going to do about it, huh?
* When you've got something this good, it only seems fair to share it around...

If you're having an affair, don't make matters
worse than they are

Convince her it was all a ghastly mistake and you'll never ever do it again.
That's what I said the last time...and the time before that...and the time
before that...
Oh.
And the time before that...and the time before that...and the time before
that...and the time before that...
Really?
And the time before that...and the time before that... I don't think she's going
to believe me.
No. I don't think she will somehow.
So, got any other bright ideas?
Tell her she should stand by you for the sake of the children...
What, our children or the one my mistress is going to have in three months'
time?
You insist on making this complicated, don't you? I'm going to ignore that.
Here are some good reasons you can suggest to your wife why she should
stand beside you in your hour of adversity:

* For the sake of the children
* Because you want to give your marriage one last try
* The Government may be toppled, letting in those awful Labour oiks
* You have discovered God
* You're begging her to, on your knees
* You'll buy her a new fur coat
* You know a top divorce lawyer who will see she gets nothing from any settlement

These reasons, on the other hand, will probably not sway her into supporting you:

* If you get thrown out of Parliament, you'll be parted from the Commons secretary you've been screwing on the side
* You'll buy her a new washing-up bowl and a pair of Marigolds
* You'll refuse to have sex with her any more if she doesn't back you
* It's a great opportunity to get her picture in the paper and make her parents proud

The press will probably ask your wife to make a statement to them. We have prepared here an ideal statement which your wife should be persuaded to repeat verbatim, selecting the most relevant answer from the choices presented:

Naturally, I was shocked to learn of my husband's affair with a model/go-go dancer/male stripper/actress/Commons researcher/secretary/marsupial/large wooden rolling pin.

I love my husband. He is a good family man, an excellent father to our one/two/three/four children and someone I both admire and look up to, despite his transgression/affair/penchant for unnatural sexual practices/injuries gained from his sexual practices/large collection of women's clothing hidden in the shed/being discovered with over 3,000 pictures cut out of the underwear pages of home shopping catalogues.

Furthermore, he has always been completely devoted to his Parliamentary work and the public good. He is an excellent MP and I do not believe that his unfaithfulness/perversions/hunger for young boys/strange to the point of absurd sexual practices/habit of appearing nude in public places in any way affects his ability to do a good job for his constituents, his Party and the nation.

I have forgiven him and I hope the nation will too. Everyone is entitled to make one/two/three/more than three/more than twenty mistakes and my husband has made his. The healing process will be long and difficult, but I know our love is strong enough to see us through.

Left to her own devices, your wife is more likely to say something like:

He's always been a lecherous disgusting little creep. The only reason we got married in the first place was because he made me pregnant and Daddy said he'd crucify him in the Conservative Party if he didn't do the decent thing.

I learned about the current affair he's been having when the rash showed up and I went to my GP. My fault for sleeping with him again, I suppose. I said the sex side of our marriage was over when I found out about him and that Welsh fly half. I agreed to carry on with this ghastly, hollow sham that I jokingly call our marriage, just so he could stay an MP and use his influence illegally to get Daddy's business some valuable building contracts. He hardly ever sees the children. He always forgets their birthdays – and often their names as well.

Now I find out he's been doing to his secretary what he and his damn Party have been doing to this country all this time. I tell you, I didn't even vote for him at the last election, because I know what he's like. Oh, and he's had crabs six times. If you watch the coverage of the Commons on television, he's the one sitting there furiously scratching his groin during Prime Minister's Question Time. They should make him Minister for Communicable Social Diseases. That's a post he'd at least know something about. Or Minister for Having it Off with Dim Little Bimbos at the Taxpayer's Expense...

So, you see how important it is to have your wife on your side when any scandal breaks. Hell hath no fury like a woman scorned...
My wife's a good sort. She'll stand by me no matter what I do.
How can you be so sure?
She's got an IQ of 86.

RESIGNATION

So this is what it all comes down to, eh?

That's entirely up to you.

It's not, is it? I mean nothing I could have done would have stopped that Sunday paper printing those photos of me and the poodle.

I suppose not...

And how could I have prevented that nun from pressing charges against me for indecent assault?

I can see that...

And that arrest for kerb-crawling...Well, how was I to know that chap with all those nipple rings I propositioned was an undercover policeman?

I can sympathise. The thing is though, if you do get convicted, you've only yourself to blame.

That's not true. I blame my lawyer. He came highly recommended. Got some chappie off a fraud charge by demonstrating that he was senile. Hey! That's an idea – maybe if I pretend I'm senile I'll get off.

I don't think so.

Hullo birds, hullo trees. Zipity doodah, Zipity ay. We will paint the bridge at midnight.

I beg your pardon.

One, two, three o'clock, four o'clock rock! I must shop for some yellow radishes...

Are you feeling all right?

At the next stroke, the time will be five...seventy-five...precisely.

Nurse! Nurse!

It's OK. It's me. I was just pretending I'm senile.

Oh. Well I don't think a jury will fall for that.

So there's only one thing left...suicide. Stand back, I've got a plastic bag and an orange and I'm not afraid to use them (in fact, I'm quite looking forward to it).

No! Put them down; that's the next section of this book. That's a last resort – we're talking here about doing the honourable thing and resigning.

Resigning?! I'd rather get beaten to within an inch of my life by one of those cat o'nine tails with metal tips on the ends!

Yes, but that's just one of the reasons you are resigning, remember?

Oh yes.

Come on, resigning's not so painful.

Is it as painful as being whipped by a cat o'nine tails with metal tips on the ends?

Er...I wouldn't have thought so.

Pity. Listen, if I resign do I get a pay-off like I would in industry. You know, a 'golden shower'?

Don't you mean 'Golden Handshake'?

Oh yes. I was thinking about something else. Anyway, why do I need advice on resigning? All I have to do is write a letter to the PM and leave it on his desk. Hey, do you think he'll try and talk me out of it?

After all you've done?

Probably not.

Listen, resigning is more complicated than that. You'll be expected to make a resignation speech at a news conference and the PM has issued certain guidelines on this.

Why?

Well, he wants to exploit your resignation. OK, you've done something so terrible you've got to go – but that doesn't stop you apologising. John Major wants your resignation to appear as part of his stand on Back to Basics. Your unmentionable acts...

They weren't unmentionable. The papers all mentioned them.

You know what I mean.

Sometimes resignation is the only answer...

What should I say in my resignation speech?

Let's see what John Major advises, shall we?

Not him again...

John Major says...

If you've done something really, really terrible and there's no option but to resign, you should be ashamed of yourself. Really you should. Every time one of you MPs does something naughty it rubs off on me. I don't mean that you literally rub something off on me. Oh no! That would be awful. And probably extremely difficult to clean off, even with a chisel, knowing what some of you get up to.

Where was I? Ah yes. If you are resigning I can recommend certain key words or phrases for your speech. These will make you look very humble and, hopefully, distance your actions from the rest of us respectable politicians:

- I'm sorry
- I'm really sorry
- I'm really, really, really sorry
- I won't do it again
- I know I've brought the good name of the Conservatives into disrepute
- My actions were in no way representative of my backbench colleagues
- My actions were in no way representative of my Cabinet colleagues
- I'm now going to leave politics forever and never even think about returning as an MP, let alone aspire to another Cabinet position like some of my infamous colleagues in the past who crept back in again after getting their secretaries in the pudding club if you know what I mean.

He seems pretty adamant that if you resign, you don't come back into his Government.

Well, you know what they say about skeletons in the cupboard.

Who told you about that? It was under the floorboards when I bought my house and yes, I know it's exactly the same height as my ex-wife, you know, the heiress, who suddenly vanished five years ago...

What are you babbling on about now?

Nothing. Nothing.

Good. Well you saw what the PM had to say about resignation speeches. To end this piece of advice here's what you should never, ever do...

These sorts of resignation speeches are expressly forbidden:

Ladies and gentlemen, due to the continuing allegations about me and two of the Gladiators I've had no alternative but to do the honourable thing and resign from this Government.

All I can say in answer to my critics was that yes, they went like express trains all night. They wouldn't let me sleep a wink. First one, then the other, then both! It was like tag-bonking! No orifice was left alone. Talk about being sore, my huge

This afternoon I resigned from my cabinet post. Not because, you understand, I'd committed a crime or acted improperly - no. I resigned because John Major wanted me to take the rap for him. You see it was him wearing that ski-mask

My distinguished colleagues, as you well know that incident involving me and that Turkish boy has hardly been out of the news all week. Well, I say 'boy' but he had a man's body alright! Anyway, all that's behind me - as was the boy - but that's another story. I try not to look back, but hey, that's the only way I could see him! This morning when I handed my resignation in to 10 Downing Street, John Major asked if that press coverage had left a nasty taste in my mouth. Well, I said, not as much as whe

Members of the press, I know most of you have come to this news conference expecting me to announce my resignation. Well, that's where you're wrong. You see I've called you all here so I can announce that the entire Conservative Cabinet are trans

As I stand here I know most of my political opponents will be glad I'm going. They're probably saying that I've had my comeuppance. That years of bedding anything in a skirt have finally caught up with me. Well, what I say is, 'Hey, I've got enough in my underpants for all the girls in the world'

SUICIDE – THE LAST HONOURABLE WAY OUT

Sometimes, the only option left open to you is to do the decent thing.

I've never done the 'decent thing' in my life. Why break the habit of a lifetime?

Suppose you've been involved in a terrible sexual scandal of awesomely perverse proportions...

Chance would be a fine thing...

Wouldn't you prefer suicide to the shame?

Nope.

Oh. But surely shame and utter humiliation is a terrible thing to endure.

Not at all, I pay perfectly good money for 'Shame and Humiliation' at Madame Josephine's every Wednesday night. It's great to be an MP!

You're just drunk on the power...

No. Actually I'm drunk on all the Bolly at the moment.

While, of course, we could not officially approve of suicide, we would expect you to conduct your final moments and the tidying up of your affairs in a way which was not detrimental to the image of the Party.

If – and of course it's entirely up to you – you do decide to take your own life rather than facing scorn and ridicule...

I pay good money for 'Scorn and Ridicule' at Madame Josephine's on Thursdays and Saturdays...

...Rather than facing scorn and ridicule, this is the sort of suicide note we would expect the police to find:

To Whom it may concern,

This is my suicide note.
   I cannot take the shame anymore. I have let down my party, my constituents, my colleagues, my family and myself.
   Please forgive me for taking my own life. I think it is best for all under the circumstances. If only I had listened to Prime Minister John Major - the finest leader this party has ever been privileged to have at the helm. A fine, decent, upstanding and thoroughly capable man, if I had only followed in his footsteps and adopted his Back to Basics policies as have 99.99% of my colleagues, it would never have come to this.
   To my darling wife, I would like to say that I always loved you and the children, ~~Toby and Jocasta~~ ~~Rodney and Jocasta~~ Rodney and Phillipa? You always meant the world to me, despite what I have been doing. The Cub Scouts meant nothing to me. Nothing, compared to the love we shared lo, these many years.
   Before I die, I would also remind the country that, under the last Labour party government, inflation, taxes, unemployment and crime levels were all far greater than they are now under the Tories.

These are suicide notes we do not want to see:

IT WAS ALL JOHN MAJOR'S FAULT!...

They're all at it! Why I got exposed I'll never know. You time will come too, you rotten bastards! I hope you choke on your Outspans!

Viva Michael Heseltine!

I claim that I've had John Major over the desk in his office, and committed numerous acts of a sexual nature with him involving Philadelphia Light Cream Cheese, a ping pong bat, two gerbils on string and a leading member of the Royal Ballet.
   Go on, prove me a liar now....

How you go is also as important as what you say when you go...

I'm not going! Let John Major do it. He's already committed political suicide. Why doesn't he go the whole hog?

He enjoys a spotless reputation.

Let me tell you now; I am not going to toss myself off over Beachy Head – unless of course there are some attractive, big-breasted women directly underneath.

John Major says...

```
                I really don't think we should be
             encouraging suicide among our MPs,
          Mr Whip.
             Resignation is the honourable thing to do
        upon exposure. I fear that this document has
        turned out somewhat extreme for my tastes,
          which, as you know, lean towards moderation in
     all things.
        I know some people say that the only good MP is
     a dead MP - the vast majority of the public, as it
     happens - but, as so many times in the past,  I
     would prefer to ignore public opinion. Lady
     Thatcher never encouraged suicide and self-
     immolation during her period in office - and
     neither will I.
```

Yes, but she was Maggie Thatcher and you're John Major. What a woman! So dominant, so strong, so in charge, so powerful; 'Mistress Maggie'...

Lady Thatcher is history...

I wish she was back; in a leather cat suit, white four-inch stilettos and a riding crop. Taking charge, grinding us all under her heels. They were such great times. We didn't need to misbehave back then. We could all fantasise about being hauled in front of her and subjected to her 'discipline'. Sexual misconduct? We didn't have the capacity for it. Just the sight and sound of her taking Neil Kinnock to pieces at Question Time and it was off to the dry cleaners for us, chum!

So that's why all these scandals are starting to break now, under the Major administration...

*Mistress Maggie... the reason for sex scandals in Mr Major's
administration (or just the cartoonist's fantasy?)*

Excuse me. I need to relieve myself urgently...my bladder that is.

You mean, if Maggie was in charge, there'd be none of these scandals?

Look, can you imagine Major handing out stern discipline?

No. He's *nice*...

*Exactly. That's why Back to Basics won't ever work. None of us can get off
on his leadership.*

I wonder if it's not too late to resign...

*Don't do that...Look, I've got one last question that I've been meaning to ask
you throughout this whole book.*

What?

Will you marry me?

I thought you'd never ask!

APPENDICES

BY JOHN MAJOR, MP

APPENDIX ONE
HOW TO BE A MODEL MP

Back to Basics is a jolly good idea, and one I am proud to be associated with as LEADER of this party. Leader; Captain; Chief; Boss; Head Honcho; Big Enchillada; The Main Man; Top Dog; Ruler; Sultan; Guv'nor; Master; Overlord; Director; Potentate.

There are those among you, I know, who believe I dreamed up Back to Basics as a way of spoiling your fun and shaming you into behaving like proper MPs ought to behave. Well, you're right – and that'll teach you to like that long-haired public school clown Michael Heseltine more than me.

If you cannot live by my Back to Basics rules, then you must resign – and good riddance to you. If, on the other hand, you wish to remain within the Party and pursue your career, you must all learn how to act like a decent human being instead of the duly elected Member of Parliament for Gomorrah North.

The purpose of this appendix is to give you some jolly useful pointers to set you off in the right direction.

The first area I want to address is hobbies. Hobbies say a lot about a man. I myself am a keen follower of cricket and Chelsea Football Club, I possess a large collection of stamps of the British Commonwealth, built up since childhood, an impressive collection of Perry Como records and am a dab hand at making Airfix kits. I can also turn my hand towards a little DIY and am particularly proud of the spice racks I have built for Norma's kitchen. When time permits, I still collect civil aircraft numbers and enjoy a spot of vegetable gardening in my allotment. I achieve all that and still fulfil my duties as leader.

These extra-curricular activities neatly fill my spare time. The devil finds use for idle hands, they say, and it is noticeable that many of you are putting said idle hands to improper uses on ladies of ill-repute, boys young enough to be your sons and all manner of fruits, vegetables and assorted implements from B & Q. Obviously you have too much spare time. I am therefore setting up a range of clubs and societies in Parliament and I expect you all to put down your names for at least three of them and attend them regularly.

These are:

The Commons Dominoes League
The Conservative Party Orienteering Society
Making nice things with balsa wood
Understanding the novels of Jane Austen
Appreciating British Wildlife [platonically]
The House Snap! Championship
Collage for beginners
Collage for intermediates
The Tony Monopoly Appreciation Society
Studying the works of Hammond Innes
The Amateur Dramatics Society
Hairdressing
The John Major Appreciation Society [Free biscuits and orange cordial]

Secondly, I wish you all to enjoy proper family lives, encompassing the 'family values' for which our Party has always stood. Here, you could do no better than to follow the example of Norma and myself. We are a blissfully happy family, sharing in many activities, including picnics, baking biscuits together, visits to Berni Steakhouses and Harvesters at least once a month, joint shopping trips, a shared interest in *Coronation Street* and regular evenings in by the fireside relaxing and listening to our cherished Tony Monopoly LP. Sometimes, we may complete a jigsaw, usually of Bavarian Castles or kittens, or indulge in a gently competitive game of Buckeroo.

When was the last time you told your wife you loved her, or that you wouldn't swop her for anyone, not even Jane Torville? I thought not! When was the last time you surprised your wife with a box of Cadbury's Roses, instead of surprising her by brazenly wearing her clothes or being caught flagrantly abusing yourself while watching a video of *Lassie Come Home*? All wives need to be told they are loved and appreciated, not 'rubbish in bed compared to that actress I just met' or 'so pig-ugly they should put themselves forward as a Labour Party candidate'.

I am jolly well fed up to my back teeth with your wives ringing me up in tears, asking me to have a 'private word' with you about your gross sexual misconduct. I will no longer cover for those of you out carousing with floozies and cheap women by telling your wives that you are working extra hours in committee or that Parliament is in a late sitting. Enough is enough.

If you are consorting with a barnyard animal, I shall jolly well tell your wife so – and to hell with the consequences!

You are in Parliament to serve the people – not to service as many of them as you can lay your hands on.

Thirdly, you could do far worse than model your budding political careers on the fine, decent, upstanding MPs of yesteryear. Like Winston Churchill. Winston Churchill and...Winston Churchill...and other ones you should go out and discover for yourselves. Or perhaps me.

Fourthly, I want you to go out and make a good impression in the newspapers. Be seen to care. Take advantage of photo opportunities

attending hospices, hospitals for sick children and poor pensioners suffering and dying because they cannot afford their fuel bills. Well, perhaps not the latter. I think you'd better avoid them – at least until the furore dies down. Speak out on popular issues – like law and order. Well, perhaps not that one, considering what a pig's ear we've made of it. Console the sick. No, on second thoughts, forget that one too.

Well, at least be seen to wear a smart suit and tie and smile a lot.

Back to Basics is our only chance to win the next general election. Yes it is. Getting rid of me won't make a blind bit of difference. Honestly. Lots of opinion polls show this. You may have missed those particular ones, but they do exist, I promise you.

To make Back to Basics work, every single one of you must become paragons of virtue. I don't care what it takes – hypnotherapy, acupuncture, aversion therapy involving electrodes to the toilet area, lots of shouting, counselling, castration, a good kicking from Norman Tebbit; I shall sanction anything I deem appropriate to bring you back into line.

Finally, I am going to introduce a new Tory Party oath of allegiance, developed by the Chief Whip's Office, which you will all be required to swear.

Please complete this sworn declaration and return it to my office at your earliest opportunity.

SWORN DECLARATION

I, the MP for......................,

agree to live by the Party's Back to Basics manifesto.
I shall be seen to love and cherish my family, no matter
how much I resent them. I shall love my wife. If I do not
have one, I will get married within six months and put
the club scene behind me forever.
    I will be faithful to my wife at all times, no matter
if I think the dopey bitch will never find me out or the
fact that I've got a hard-on like the Telecom Tower.
    I will act respectably in everything I do and say. I
will throw away any Bronski Beat and Farmyard Noises
albums in my possession and choose to play only classical
music and easy listening from this moment on.
    I shall treat my children with respect. I shall learn
their names and ages, remember their birthdays, encourage
their education and not ask their friends to play games

- 114 -

of 'nude blind man's buff' at parties, nor the infamous 'catch my wad' game which has been the ruination of many a promising career.

I will dress respectably at all times, even when I think people will not see me. Any underwear garments made of lace, rubber, PVC, leather, the finely spun and woven pubic hair of Bolivian peasants, or those lacking crotches in any way in my possession will be immediately and discreetly disposed of. I will bin them or burn them, not donate them to my local Oxfam shop, enter into 'swoppsies' with a fellow backbencher or try to sell them through the pages of 'Exchange and Mart'.

I will eat fruit, because it is good for me – and that is the only relationship I shall have with it.

I will not accidentally strangle myself in some sad, perverted auto-erotic enterprise and bring shame upon the Party.

The only watersports I shall indulge in are swimming, windsurfing, water skiing and canoeing.

I will not spread vicious rumours about my fellow MPs, just because they got that tasty new researcher into bed and she laughed at me when I tried it on with her.

I will not accept backhanders – in the financial or sexual sense.

I will continue to support John Major as the leader of this Party, no matter what I may personally think of his abilities, policies, or common grammar school upbringing.

Signed..

Witnessed..

Dated..

APPENDIX TWO
WHAT I'M GOING TO DO IF
YOU DON'T BEHAVE

Sometimes I can get really, really angry. Oh yes!

I hope all you MPs have found this guide interesting and informative and that you'll follow all the advice in it.

If you don't I'll be very angry. Very angry indeed. In fact, I'll be so angry I might even lose my temper. This, as Norma will inform you, is not a pretty sight. She still shudders when she remembers the day she accidentally squeezed the toothpaste from the middle of the tube. I still get really annoyed just thinking about that.

Anyway, if I find out you're misbehaving, like if you've been out on the tiles, galavanting with some floozie when you should have been enjoying a cup of Ovaltine and a round of whist with your wife, my retribution will be really unpleasant.

If you're in my Cabinet you'll face the full force of my wrath. For a start, when it comes to the mid-morning tea and coffee at Number 10 I'll withhold your biscuits! You think I'm joking, don't you? But I really mean it. I do. Picture the scene if you will. We've just finished struggling through the latest EC crisis when the tea trolley comes in. I will then act in my executive capacity and commandeer the biscuit barrel under the Emergency Powers act.

Now I've known you all long enough to know your personal favourites. For example, Douglas Hurd likes bourbons; Michael Howard likes Garibaldis; Kenneth Clarke likes those iced ones with different sports on the back; Michael Heseltine likes Jammy Dodgers and chocolate fingers (the greedy devil); Peter Lilley likes those Nice biscuits (and gets all those sugary crumbs all over the table) and not forgetting Michael Portillo who likes Chocolate Hob Nobs (as do I).

How would it feel if I denied you your favourite biscuits, gentlemen? Not very pleasant, is it? So just bear that in mind next time you're thinking of committing some indiscretion.

And as for the rest of you MPs out there. Well, I might not be aware of your taste in biscuits (apart from Sir Marcus Fox, who I know likes a Kit Kat – as in fact do most of the 1922 Committee) but it doesn't matter. I can still be very unpleasant.

For starters, if I see you in the corridor I won't even say good morning to you (or good afternoon, if it's afternoon. Or good evening, if it's evening, come to that). No, sir. What's more, as soon as I've walked past you I'll turn and put my tongue out – or, worse still, blow a great big raspberry and everyone else in the corridor will know that you've been up to no good.

If you've *really* made me mad I might ring you up from my office and when you answer, put the phone down. Or even stick a small piece of notepaper saying 'Kick Me' on to your back when you least suspect it!

From reading this I hope you'll know just how strongly I feel about Back to Basics – and the lengths I am prepared to go to in order to make my views felt within the Party.

You have been warned!

This is a list of the things that really, really annoy me so you can judge for
yourself how volatile I can be.

The things that really, really annoy me – by John Major

- Tory MPs involved in sex scandals
- Tory MPs involved in any other form of scandal
- Squeezing the toothpaste from the middle
- Putting toilet paper on the holder the wrong way round (i.e. so that it
  hangs near to the wall)
- Cars parked in bus lanes
- Any other form of discourtesy to road users
- Euro rebels
- Leaving lights on unnecessarily
- Not closing doors behind you
- Squeezing the toothpaste from the middle (it makes me so angry I
  had to list it again)
- Torville and Dean not getting that gold medal
- People who take one bite out of a biscuit, decide they don't like it,
  and put it back in the barrel for me to eat later
- Dropping litter
- People who call Michael Heseltine 'Tarzan' like he's some sort of
  hunky sex-god (he's more like 'Cheetah' if you ask me!)
- People who don't wipe their feet before coming in
- Eating on public transport – and the intrusive playing of personal
  stereos
- Leaving the tops off biros so they dry out
- Not washing your hands after you go to the toilet
- People saying I'm not an effective leader
- Opinion polls

APPENDIX THREE
FINDING THE PERFECT MATE

If all you philandering MPs out there had a perfect partner – you know, the sort of little lady who's good at cooking, always remembers birthdays, knows what biscuits you like, can darn socks, is loyal, trustworthy and faithful – and not too demanding when it comes to 'bedroom business', then there wouldn't be any need for this book, would there?

It's only because you haven't found her that you're dallying around ladies of ill repute and getting up to all sorts of monkey business. Now you all know Norma and what a lovely wife she is. In all the time we've been married I've never had a naughty thought for another woman (well, only once and that was for Jane Torville – but that just shows I am human after all).

Anyway, the point I am trying to make is that you could all do worse than follow my example of how I found my true love:

JOHN MAJOR'S GUIDE TO COURTING

To win the heart of a fair maiden it's really important to woo her in the right way. In my experience the way to a woman's heart is through poetry and music. What I say is never underestimate the power of the written word (well, and the sung word, although it is written down in the first place, of course).

Anyway I used both of these methods when I was courting my nearest and dearest, Norma. All you MPs out there are probably wondering what's the secret of my success with women. Not that I'm seeing lots of women, you understand. Well I am seeing them, in the ocular sense – I'm not seeing them in the sense of going on smoochy dates with them, if you see what I mean.

All ladies love romance and poetry – so what better than to combine them in a romantic poem. Of course, you can copy one straight out of a poetry book, but that's not very original and it might indicate a lack of commitment (if you do this, use a Shakespearean sonnet. Try to avoid 'Jabberwocky', 'Dulce Et Decorum Est' and 'The Night Mail').

It's much more entertaining to compose your own poems to the lady of your life, but be careful, it's not as easy as it may sound. So you can see what sort of approach works, here are some poems I wrote to Norma when we started stepping out together:

JOHN AND NORMA

To N.
Roses are red
Violets are blue
I love you a lot
Yes I do
From J. XXXX

Norma, darling
You shaved my biscuits
You shaved my life
Now I want you
To be my wife
John XXX

Dear Norma,
    If you should ever leave me
It would be most disagreeable

John XXXX

Norma,
    Your lips are like rubies
    Your skin is like gold
    I hope you don't think
    i'm being too bold.
    All my love (oh yes!) John XX

Norma, my dear
    Like a choice of biscuits you present quite a riddle
    Like a custard cream, you're soft in the middle
    Like a Jammy Dodger, your lips are red
    When we are married, we can go to bed
Love John XXXX
    (Please don't show your mother this one)

I know it's hard to believe that an aggressive and assertive leader like myself has a sensitive side but it's true. And I'm not ashamed of it, either. If you're not sensitive, it's best to avoid poetry as a form of expression. However, if you are determined (and I admire perseverance as a personal trait) this might be really useful to you:

Subjects for love poetry

Good:
- Flowers
- Birds
- The seasons
- Love eternal
- Anything that portrays your beloved as a beautiful, kind, caring and considerate person

Bad:
- Insects
- Rude parts of your body
- The exchange of bodily fluids
- Industrial smelting (including the Bessemer Process)
- Roy Hattersley
- Violent crime
- The sixteen girls you previously dated

MUSIC

Do you know who said, 'If music be the food of love, play on'? No? Well I don't either. But at least I've got an excuse – I only went to grammar school. Anyway, whoever it was hit the nail right on its head.

We chaps can use the right sort of music to, dare I say it, get the ladies in the mood for a bit of smooching. (Now how's that for some free advice?)

I like to think of music as poetry set to a tune (I'm quite good at abstract thinking such as this). As you'd probably guess, the best music for this sort of thing is slow and what I call 'lovey-dovey'. As a guide, use records by the artistes I've listed below (I'm a bit out of touch with the hit parade but you should find them in most record shops).

Using music to set the mood

John Major's recommended artistes for intimate candlelit dinners:

- Andy Williams
- Tony Bennett
- The Mike Sammes Singers
- Acker Bilk
- Howard Keel
- Tony Monopoly
- Perry Como
- James Last
- Tony Orlando and Dawn

I hope poetry and music prove to be as successful for you as they were for me. If they're not, for whatever reason, then there is another way to find your perfect partner. It's a service I've been running from Number 10 in my spare time for almost a year now (actually, Norma helps me with the paperwork).

It's called JOHN MAJOR'S MATE LINE and, if you're at all interested, fill in this form and post it back to me. Remember, confidentiality is assured at all times (or rather it would be, but I haven't received any replies yet).

JOHN MAJOR'S MATE LINE

ATTENTION ALL LONELY MPs!

Are you really happy chasing after loose bits of fluff and having sexual relations with a different girl almost every week? Don't you wish you could settle down with a nice 'Little Lady' and have a quiet and pleasant home life like me?

Well, if your answer's YES, welcome to John Major's Mate Line. We promise to match you up with any number of lovely ladies on our computer - all selected from local Party offices and Young Conservative Associations up and down the country. (If your answer's NO, then I'm disappointed in you and recommend that you jolly well think again.)

What's more, the service is provided free of charge. I think it goes to show that I really do have your interests at heart

(that's actually a rather clever pun, even if I do say so
myself).

Name..

Age...

Constituency...

Who of the following most resembles your ideal partner?

❑ Norma (but remember, she's already spoken for!)
❑ Douglas Hurd's wife
❑ That nice lady from the Shake 'n Vac advert
❑ Katie Boyle
❑ Jane Torville
❑ Sue Lawley
❑ That girl who plays Cassandra in 'Only Fools & Horses'
❑ That girl in the Dateline ad. You know, the one with the white
Argyll sweater and the squint
❑ Patricia Routledge
❑ Deirdre Barlow

Now for a question just to see how red-blooded you really are!!!

How often would you envisage having a bit of slap and tickle?

❑ Once every other week (you must be of Mediterranean
extraction!)
❑ Once a month
❑ Once every Parliamentary session
❑ On the occasion of the Queen's speech
❑ When you want to have children
❑ When Chelsea win away
❑ Less frequent

OK John, I've got nothing to lose! Fix me up with the girl of my
dreams.

P.S. If it comes to a leadership challenge I'll be backing you!

Signed ....

Send completed form back to:
John Major's Mate Line c/o 10 Downing Street, London SW1

APPENDIX FOUR
A MESSAGE TO MY WOMEN MPs

Crikey! We're nearly at the end of the book and I've just realised I haven't really addressed the women MPs in my Party! It's lucky I've got a few pages left or I'd be most upset at overlooking all you lovely ladies!

Anyway, this section is for you. If there's any men reading you'd better put the book down now. There's nothing interesting here so you'd be better off watching *World In Action,* reading back issues of Hansard or whatever you do to unwind. That's it. Go away.

Good. It's just me and you ladies, and I must say, what a delightful bunch of girls you all are. I wish my Party consisted entirely of women. Yes I do. Not that I'm implying that I want to be surrounded by women just so I can accidentally brush against you in the crowded division lobby. Not at all. I intended that statement to be quite without innuendo, you understand (not that I'd be offended, mind you, if anyone *did* accidentally brush up against me, particularly that MP – I can't remember her name – but she looks a bit like Jane Torville).

Anyway, where was I? Oh yes. What I was trying to say was that you ladies are far less trouble than your male counterparts. Do you know, I was pleasantly surprised the way it's all worked out. Really. When I took over as leader of the Conservative Party I was a bit worried that you'd all have to leave early before an important vote so you could pick the kids up from school or prepare dinner.

Or that you'd have to keep rushing to the bathroom in the middle of an important debate; or burst into tears if your Private Member's bill fails its Second Reading. Fortunately it hasn't been like that at all. And the times we do argue, like over current Government policy, I just excuse it because it's your 'time of the month'. Don't worry ladies – I'm a modern man and I can make allowances for our biological differences.

I even thought that, as women, you'd only be interested in topics like health and education – and be upset because there was no Select Committee on babies or shopping – or even Steve McQueen – but I was very pleased to be proved wrong. No. I can quite categorically put my hand on my heart and say 'Hooray for the women in my Government. Hooray! Hooray!'

Now, ladies, you understand the problem I've been having with most of my male MPs. I expect they act like your husbands. Always looking for a bit of nookie on the side – not that I'm in any way implying that your husbands are unfaithful. That would be the last thing I wanted to suggest. No, I'm sure you and your husbands are fulfilled in the bedroom department and there's no need for him to stray. Not that I ever think about what you and your husband get up to in the bedroom. No. I never think about that at all. Really I don't. Thinking of you in your boudoir is one of the furthest thoughts from my mind.

Anyway, what I'm leading up to is asking for your assistance in trying to keep my male MPs in line. The Whip's Office is trying its hardest to teach them the right way to behave but the feminine touch wouldn't go amiss.

You see, it's my belief that my male MPs wouldn't be hell-bent on defying my Back to Basics philosophy if they had a mother's influence nearby. And that's where you come in.

Now I wasn't thinking of you breast-feeding them – heavens no! Though I'm sure that thought's crossed their smutty public school minds on many an occasion. Nor was I thinking about you wiping their bottoms when they've finished on the toilet (and I dare say this thought has even crossed a few of their minds as well, the dirty so-and-sos). I'm not even talking about tying their gloves through the sleeves of their jackets with elastic or turning up with their wellington boots when it's raining.

No. What I was thinking of was whether you could offer some motherly advice to them to keep them in line. Men have a subconscious desire to obey their mothers so this idea of mine just might work.

These are the sorts of things you should say to them if you know they're getting up to naughty mischief.

'What do you want to go out with her for?'
'Don't do that, you'll go blind'
'If your father knew what you were up to it would break his heart'
'You treat this House like a hotel!'
'You're not going out 'till you've done your constituency business'
'You could do a lot better than her'
'I want you back here by ten o'clock'
'You're not going anywhere with hands like that!'
'Don't say that, dear. It's not nice'
'Any more of that and I'll send you to your room!'

IMPORTANT: Whatever you do, resist the temptation (for obvious reasons) to say, 'You're not too old to put across my knee and spank!'

One additional thing you might like to do is offer to do their ironing for them. They'd be so worried about you turning up without warning at their London flat, they'd probably spend the whole time clearing the place up. In any case, they wouldn't dare invite girlfriends round for a bit of nookie in case you barged in on them. Clever, eh? They don't call me cunning John Major for nothing you know!

Anyway, that's all for me now. Thank you for reading this, ladies. I'd better let you go now as I'm certain you'll have some sewing or laundry to do.

GRATEFUL ACKNOWLEDGMENTS

Many people have assisted in the compilation of this guide. Foremost among them are my two very good friends Mark Leigh & Mike Lepine. Long and hard they laboured over this volume with me, burning the midnight oil and sharing the camaraderie of my biscuit barrel (Mark likes Penguins while Mike prefers McVities plain chocolate digestives which he can dunk in milk).

They have written ten previous saucy and amusing tomes such as *How To Be A Complete Bastard* (one for Michael Heseltine, I think), *How To Be A Complete Bitch* (ditto), The *Official Politically Incorrect Handbook* (not to be confused with our manifesto) and sundry others which, along with many others in this nation, I keep in the lavatory.

The cartoons were supplied by a very nice man called Larry (he wouldn't divulge his surname but I do know he has a penchant for chocolate fingers). He's drawn pictures in lots of books and has an autobiography out called *Larry on Larry* which I am told is most amusing.

I would be remiss if I did not mention the sterling research work of Philippa Hatton (who could be tempted by almond shortbread), the tolerance of Debbie Leigh (who wouldn't say no to a Jaffa Cake, although I'm not certain whether this is technically a biscuit or a cake), Neville & Gill Landau (who both derive great pleasure from Gingernuts – as indeed does Glenys Kinnock – ho, ho), Ian 'Pass me a Wagon Wheel' Marshall, Roger 'I don't actually like biscuits' Houghton and last, but certainly not least, my dear lady wife Norma (who's partial to the odd custard cream).

John

John (make mine a Chocolate Hob Nob) Major